# The Cape Breton Giant
## and Other Writings

*James D. Gillis.*

# GIANT!
## WONDER of WONDERS!
### TOM THUMB ECLIPSED

A NGUS M'KASKILL, the Nova Scotia GIANT, is now holding his Levees in Halifax, at MASON HALL, at 3 o'clock, P. M., and in the evening at 7 o'clock.

This wonderful Boy was born in Lewis, the largest of the Western Scottish Isles, and came to this country when at the age of 3 years. Since then he has resided in St. Ann's Parish, Cape Breton. Until past 12 years he was considered a DWARF.

He is only 19 years old, weighs nearly 400 pounds, 7 feet 7 inches high. He is remarkably well formed and proportioned, and when he arrives at his full growth will exhibit Herculanean feats of Strength. He will only remain in HALIFAX for a few days. Admission 1s.3d., Children half price. Pay at the door.

—S. Dunseith

Angus MacAskill, the Cape Breton Giant, and James D. Gillis, Author and Teacher, in a composite photo created by Carol Kennedy

# The
# Cape Breton
# GIANT
## and
## Other Writings

### James D. Gillis

featuring "A Memoir of James D. Gillis"
by Thomas H. Raddall

PHOTOGRAPHS

**Breton Books**
Wreck Cove

Editor: Ronald Caplan
Production Assistant: Bonnie Thompson
Composition: Glenda Watt

Our thanks to the University Archives, Dalhousie University Library, Thomas H. Raddall Papers, for Mr. Raddall's "Halifax Revisited—A Memoir of James D. Gillis." Thanks to Dr. Gwendolyn Davies who supplied poems and comments from *The Song Fishermen's Song Sheet*, and to Brenda Grantmyre for permission to offer her mother's correspondence with James D. Gillis. Lauchlin MacNeil's ballad is from *Cape Breton Humor,* ed. Stuart McCawley (1929); a version with tune is in *Songs and Stories from Deep Cove Cape Breton,* ed. Ronnie MacEachern (1979). Continued thanks to Michelle Cavanaugh and the staff of The Giant MacAskill Museum at Englishtown.

Photos on pages vi, viii, x, 94, courtesy Beaton Institute collection, University College of Cape Breton. Photos on pages xii, 72, and 98 are courtesy the Photography Collection, Public Archives of Nova Scotia. William Arthur Deacon's writing is offered wiith the permission of Richard Landon, Director, Thomas Fisher Rare Book Library, University of Toronto. Thanks to Dr. John Lennox, York University, for his help with Deacon information, and to Judge Denne Burchell for his shared interest in James D. Gillis, and his continued encouragement.

Canada Council   Conseil des Arts
for the Arts     du Canada

We acknowledge the support of
the Canada Council for the Arts for our publishing program.

We also acknowledge support from Cultural Affairs,
Nova Scotia Department of Tourism and Culture

**NOVA SCOTIA**
Tourism and Culture

**National Library of Canada Cataloguing in Publication**
Gillis, Jas. D. (James Donald), b. 1870

The Cape Breton giant : and other writings / James D. Gillis, author ; Ronald Caplan, editor ; with portions by Thomas H. Raddall ... [et al.].

ISBN 1-895415-80-2

1. Gillis, Jas. D. (James Donald), b. 1870. 2. MacAskill, Angus, 1825-1863. I. Caplan, Ronald, 1942- II. Raddall, Thomas H., 1903-1994. III. Title.

PS8513.I6A12 2002      C818'.409      C2002-905679-9
PR9199.3.G5417A12 2002

# The
# Cape Breton
# GIANT

## A Truthful Memoir

# by James D. Gillis

# A Brief Sketch

THE AUTHOR to give a sketch, a brief one, of his own life, by way of introduction to those of his readers with whom he has not the honor of being acquainted.

I was born on July 11th, 1870, at Strathlorne, not far from the residence of John MacIsaac, Donald's son.

In early childhood I removed, or more correctly was removed, to Upper Margaree. I went to school some there, and later on became proficient enough to teach school. By the way, my teachers were Jane Gillis, D. M. MacFarlane, Maggie H. Gillis, Malcolm H. Gillis, James MacFarlane, Flora M. Gillis, Archibald D. MacFarlane, Dan MacPhail and A. S. MacDougall.

I was twice to the United States; I do not say so for the sake of boast.

I am at present engaged in school-teaching in Kiltarlity school.

This Book is Dedicated
To My Friend
JOHN M. MACLEAN
of Scotsville

Gentleman of More than Ordinary Merit

MacAskill family homestead at Englishtown, St. Ann's Bay

# PREFACE
## By their Biographies

THE CELEBRITIES OF OTHER LANDS are daily brought before our eyes. This is well, for it's pleasant, recreative and beneficial to know and to study the lives of great men. The poet Longfellow says:

> "Lives of great men all remind us
> We can make our lives sublime;
> And departing leave behind us
> Foot prints on the sands of time."

Longfellow is right. Experience is an able teacher moreover, and we can actually derive benefit from the story of the ways and means by which the great overcame difficulties, and acquired fortune and fame and attained to eminence.

Plutarch said: "To be ignorant of the lives of the most celebrated men of antiquity is to continue in a state of childhood all our days."

Now, dear reader, is it not proper to perpetuate the fame of a deserving country?

> "Breathes there a man with soul so dead,
> Who never to himself has said:
> This is my own, my native land,
> Whose heart had ne'er within him burned
> As home his footsteps he has turned?"

Cape Bretonians, one and all, remember that Angus Mac-Askill was our countryman. Remember that we have reason to be proud of him. Remember that he was one of the greatest giants the world has ever seen. Yes, one of the giants of the world was a native of Cape Breton.

But apart from our hero's bodily strength—he was also an excellent man otherwise. The following stanza is suggestive of his general personal character.

> "True worth is in being, not seeming;
> Some little good—not in the dreaming
> Of great things to do by and by,
> For whatever may be said in blindness
> and in spite of fancies of youth,

There's nothing so kingly as kindness,
And nothing so royal as truth."

The writing of this work was suggested by Murdoch MacLean, of Upper East Ainslie. The author had seen an article in the "Family Herald and Weekly Star" about Angus MacAskill. In a colloquy which this suggested, Mr. MacLean said, "It would be a grand idea to write a life of MacAskill." The author soon took up the matter, and this book is the result.

The author desires to thank the following people for their help: Kenneth P. MacKay, Rear Scotsville; Duncan MacAskill, St. Ann's; John A. Morrison, S. Gut, St. Ann's; Alick MacKinnon, North Ainslie; John P. MacKay, Scotsville; Hugh Gillis, Warden, Upper Margaree; John H. MacPhail, Upper E. Ainslie.

He also desires to thank Murdoch C. MacLean of North Ainslie, for suggestions.

Respectfully,

James D. Gillis, Teacher

One of the Giant's sisters in the front room of the family home

# INTRODUCTION

There is not a settlement in the Dominion of Canada, or in the United States, that is not aware of the fact that there once lived a man by the name of Angus MacAskill, who was a prodigy of size and strength. This general idea, my friends, is not enough; it is rather vague to be satisfactory. True it is that in some settlements a story or two may be heard, but again, this is not enough.

Now this book gives all the important events of MacAskill's career in language which, if sometimes florid, is none the less easily understood by all who are fairly versed in the language of England.

The reader may have heard different or deviating versions of some of the exploit anecdotes here furnished. She or he may perhaps doubt the authenticity of this book, but the author is satisfied that this work is virtually a superb representative of MacAskill's greatness.

The author's researches for information were thorough. Now he ventures to say that a few readings of this life and exploits of Angus MacAskill are emphatically enough to enable any person to grasp a nonshadowy conception of the hero. Moreover, he believes that these readings will be pleasurable, recreative, very instructive, and practically beneficial.

As an "inspiring volume," it will possibly be of benefit to old and young. The language being easy as already stated, no one need fail to derive morals from the life of MacAskill, which may permanently profit.

Geographical descriptions are profusely given. These are almost essential. Old and later day history further illuminates the reader's path to the knowledge he seeks, a thorough knowledge of the Cape Breton Giant.

The fact that, as a rule, only one exploit is portrayed in each chapter makes the reading of this book far from tiresome. The memory is not overtaxed, and at the close thereof "all draw long breaths and hope that another rapid is near." The above quotation is from the illustrious writer, Principal Grant. It is used in a metonymical sense, of course.

The author is confident that it will be found more interesting than a fairy tale. He has devoted some time to the work, having commenced it in the winter of 1898 at Upper East Ainslie.

Applicable quotations sparkle here and there, and where convenient are credited to their authors.

Simon MacRitchie, a local merchant, and Angus MacAskill's brother, John, wearing the Giant's vest. Note the Giant's boot. The most complete collection of Giant Angus MacAskill artifacts is housed at The Giant MacAskill Museum, operated by The Giant MacAskill Heirs Association, at Englishtown on beautiful St. Ann's Bay, Victoria County, Cape Breton Island.

# Chapter I

# Birth Place of MacAskill

ON THE WEST COAST of Scotland is a cluster of islands, called the Hebrides, about five hundred in number, of which one hundred are inhabited. Some of the islands have high mountains, and are noted for their picturesque scenery. The climate is mild and humid. The Hebrides are divided by an arm of the sea called the Little Minch into the Inner Hebrides and the Outer Hebrides.

The inner group lies close to the west of Scotland. The principal islands which constitute the group are: Skye, Mull, Jura, Islay, Arran, Bute and Staffa. The latter is a small island on the west of Mull, and is remarkable for its basaltic columns, and for Fingal's cave.

Fingal's cave, to the Irish and Scotch people, how musical the name! for it recalls to memory what we have learned of the great Fingal, an illustrious king of a part of Scotland in the days of antiquity. Yes, and reminds us of his other sons, Gall, Conman and Oscar, also "famous in story." Fingal and his sons, in their own way, were like bonny Marshall Ney of France, "the bravest of the brave," and we have no reason to conclude that they were likewise reputed the greatest of the great. They were generous, chivalrous and brave.

Ossian's poetic narration of his visit to Erin or Ireland cannot be excelled. Ossian was romantic. The maids of Scot-

1

land were beautiful and charming, yet none of them approached to Ossian's idea of womenkind. Fingal saw and smiled and said, "My son, go to Ireland, there is many a lovely maiden there, and I believe you will see one at least there who will more than captivate your youthful heart." Ossian went. He arrived at the palace of an Irish King, where he got a hospitable reception. It chanced that on the very day, the King's daughter, the fairest maid of Erin, was to be given in marriage to the best duelist. The arms used were a shield and spear. Ossian won the day though there were several competitors, and this princess gave him her hand with her heart in it, and his joy on that day he remembered till his dying day.

It must not be omitted that, previous to the duel or contest of spears, the heroes were permitted to get a glimpse of the lovely princess. Ossian was so enamoured by her beauty that he was willing, were it possible, to die for her hand ten thousand times.

However, he returned to Scotland soon after accompanied by his wife. They lived in bliss for many a year, but cruel death at length robbed him of his darling "Evir Aluinn."

Iona contains the ruins of a monastery, a famed seat of learning, where Calum Cile, otherwise known as St. Columba, presided and taught in the days of "lang syne." Eigg is famed for the cave of Frances in which all the inhabitants of the island were smoked to death by a hostile clan.

The outer group of the Hebrides comprises Lewis, North Uist, Benbecula, South Uist, Barra, and numerous smaller islands. They are separated by narrow passages, and extend in a line of about one hundred and twenty miles in length. The total population of the Hebrides is 1,000,000 —(See *J.B. Calkin's Gen. Geography.*)

The South-west part of Lewis is called Harris—here our illustrious hero, Angus MacAskill, was born. As an infant, he was, as said elsewhere, but of average size and nobody dreamt of the bustle his future prodigious size and appalling strength were to occasion throughout the whole world, civilized and uncivilized, from pole to pole.

But, reverting to Harris, be it said that it has produced many eminent men, and forefathers of eminent men, and though many of them "were born to blush unseen" and to "waste their sweetness on the desert air," yet, generally speaking, the Harrissonians and their descendants of other climes rang high.

Angus MacAskill was born in the year 1825. His parents were respectable, and of "blood unstained and lineage good."

His father was 5 ft. 9 in. in height, and stout. His mother was a good sized woman. There was a family of twelve besides him, three girls and nine boys. There were two girls and a boy older than he. Four of his brothers and two of his sisters are still living. Some of the family died in infancy.

## Chapter II

# Cape Breton As It Is

CAPE BRETON ISLAND is to the north-west of the peninsula of Nova Scotia. It is divided into four counties, namely: Inverness, Victoria, Cape Breton and Richmond.

Cape Breton Island is remarkable for its beautiful scenery. Good harbors are plentiful. It has a plenitude of good highways and some railways. Of the latter kind of accommodation, many more are talked about, and the expectations of those interested may be gratified all in good time. The soil is generally fertile, and is extensively cultivated. The fisheries on and off the coast waters are famous. The

Bras d'Or lakes and some fresh water lakes, as Ainslie, are simply enchanting. Into the latter flows Trout River—a favorite resort of trout. From Lake Ainslie flows the South-West of Margaree River, a river, though fairly large, still unassuming, a river whose intrinsic loveliness, coupled with still more charming surroundings, has a prominent place in the directory of superb phenomena. Reverting to Lake Ainslie, it is sufficient to say that a great writer has successfully demonstrated that it is equal in beauty to the paragons of such beauties, viz., the Killarney Lakes of Ireland. Again, Middle River, Harvard Lakes, North-East Margaree, Cheticamp, Broad Cove, Mabou, Port Hood, Judique, Nyanza, Baddeck, Whycocomagh, the Sydneys, East Bay, Mira, Arichat, St. Peters, and St. Ann's possess panoramas of scenic magnificence universally supposed to be unrivalled beyond our shores.

The island is entering a "career of brilliant promise." The exodus to other parts is decreasing. The flow of our boys and girls to the United States will probably cease forever at no distant day. The average Cape Bretonian is a George Washington in the line of truthfulness. But that Dingley Bill of the Americans indirectly contributes to Cape Breton's coffers. The resources of our island are many. It invariably pays to develop them. Many, many reasons could be adduced to prove that it is far better for the Cape Bretonians to stay at home than to go abroad, and of late years experience has confirmed the majority and more than those who have been fortunate enough to gain a foothold in Cape Breton Island cannot have it for a better land upon this revolving star that we inhabit.

Before "you and I were young," Cape Breton Island belonged to France. Vivacious France was "quick to learn and wise to know" the great value of Isle Royale as they called Cape Breton. They built a town on the east coast fortified "to kill" and called it Louisbourg in honor of the then King Louis of France.

4

Louisbourg's fortifications were not kept in good repair. In 1745 A.D., it was taken by a small fleet from Great Britain and an army of New Englanders. France was bereft of Isle Royale. Afterwards it was ceded to France. Again, in 1758, however, Louisbourg was finally captured by Great Britain. The bon Isle Royale was ceded forever to Great Britain in 1763 A.D.

From 1784 to 1819 A.D. the island formed a separate province, under military Government.

While a military Government would not be adequate today, it is clear it would be much better for the island to be, still and forever, a separate province. With due respect to the inhabitants of the peninsula, we are satisfied that it adds nothing to our dignity at home or abroad to be affiliated with them under one provincial Government. As for roads and bridge grants, etc., there is a "leagued oppression" against Cape Breton in these matters, which needs no Argus to observe. However, there is a sentiment among the islanders in favor of secession. At a seasonable opportunity a "long, strong pull together" will gain for us that separation which will be the keystone to our political freedom.

In closing this chapter, it may be remarked that, as the climate of our island is grand that it is reasonable to suppose that MacAskill, the hero of our tale, owed some of his size and strength to his being bred here for the most part. Yes, our island is exceptionally conducive to growth of humanity. A visit to us will convince anyone of this. While we admit that our hero was by far the greatest of all, the average Cape Bretonian is little less than a giant, comparatively speaking, but the debts we owe our land we shall remember, our gratitude our land esteems full high, hence while Cape Breton exists, she will reverberate with praise of her sons and the realm of size and strength vaunt our hero to the very skies. Such, such will Cape Breton show her love of him who loved her well.

# Chapter III

# MacAskill Comes Across

WHEN MACASKILL was a youth, the subject of immigration to America was pervaded with great and sometimes unrealized expectations. Of course, truth is stranger than fiction, and a truthful account of America could not be exceeded in wonders and interest by the most fabulous writer orator. Yet, there is no clime on earth where all succeed. Even America is not an exception, though it offers the poor exceptional chances. Hence it was that many immigrants even from Scotland were disappointed. But it is gratifying to know that the great majority who crossed the Atlantic's roar to the land of the setting sun might reasonably celebrate the day the thoughts of coming over flashed through their minds.

In those days America was the Boston, the Whycocomagh or the Klondike of to-day. News from America excited public interest to concert pitch. In truth, a vessel hailing from the New World would occasion as lively a bustle as did the arrival of Sir Randolph Murray, with his "News of Battle," after the Battle of Flodden. As favorable reports were usually submitted, it is no marvel that many "took a leap and o'er the sea."

Moreover, the Scottish islands, as well as other parts of Europe, were becoming overcrowded. The resources of these countries were seldom equal to the demands made upon them. In many cases, in spite of economy, thrift and hard labour, "want even as an armed man came down upon their sheds."

It may not be irrelevant here to remark what incalculable gratitude the greater part of the civilized world owes Spain. Were it not for Spain, America might not have been yet discovered. True it is that Columbus was not a Spaniard, but it is equally true that it was Spain that furnished him the means to cross.

Say, reader, just think of the millions who have been indebted thus to Spain for fame, fortune and life itself. Fancy the thousands who, of recent years, came from Europe, combined with the millions whose forefathers came from there, yes, fancy them, packed, I may say, in Europe; who can picture the result? As long as an inhabitant of America appreciates elbow room and pure air, he or she is lacking some way if Spain is not recalled to memory with a flash of gratitude.

Yet there are some, but in the honest Dominion of Canada their ranks are wearing thinner, who would rejoice in the downfall of Spain. The same people would laud their own little idol of humanity to the skies—these little idols of theirs whose prominence falls like that of kites, and likewise would fall to be lost forever only for the tangent selfishness by which it is fastened to some unscrupulous hand.

It is of little interest to refer to that discovery of America by the Northmen. It was at best a slipshod affair, and resulted in songs which our ordinary people of this day could not understand.

As for Cabot and others, previous to Columbus' discovery, they had never dreamt of the roundness or rotundity of the earth.

But our great benefactor, Columbus, studied physiography for years. At length he concluded that the earth was round. He set off westerly for East India. By the way, though confident in his conclusions about the earth's form, he was not aware that there was such a country as America. Yes, he set off for India, but better still, instead of discovering a shorter route to that land than the one then taken, he discovered the land of lands, America.

But enough. However, when Angus MacAskill was six years old he saw the ship that brought him o'er. Yes, he was but six years old when his parents led him by the hand to the ship. Though his parents were confident in the future, yet their hearts were almost bursting as they bade their friends a "heart-warm fond adieu." Angus shed tears, too. Next morning the ship left the harbour. When Angus realized that they were actually going to live out of sight of the old home, he cried bitterly. His parents consoled him as well as they could, but almost in vain.

However, as was customary, when the vessel proceeded out a piece, twelve violinists stood at the stern. Soothed by this sprightly air, Angus dried his tears. By and by, he pouted, "I'll be a man yet, and may yet see my own, my native land," and he did see the country of his birth, which may be credited to some extent to his determined will.

This may possibly remind some of Napoleon Bonaparte at the Bridge of Lodi. 'Twas at the Bridge of Lodi, during an exciting engagement with the Austrians, that the idea flashed through Napoleon Bonaparte's mind that he might yet be a great man.

However, after an otherwise uneventful voyage, Angus MacAskill arrived safely at St. Ann, Victoria County, Cape Breton Island.

## Chapter IV

# From Upper Margaree to St. Ann's

A JOURNEY FROM UPPER MARGAREE to St. Ann's gives pleasure, recreation and benefit. It can be more conveniently and profitably preformed in summer or autumn.

Leaving Upper Margaree the tourist ascends to Egypt. Egypt is a fine settlement, physically and otherwise. It is fairly well adapted to farming.

Not far from Egypt is Piper's Glen, where a famous piper, Neil Jamieson, dwells. In regard to pipers and violinists, Cape Breton is not behind. Hector MacQuarrie of Loch Ban; John N. Jamieson, formerly of Broad Cove; a Mr. Beaton, of Mabou; the MacKinnons' pipers of bonny Lake Ainslie; Allan J. MacFarlane, Duncan Gillis, James Hugh Gillis, and the intellectual giant, Malcolm H. Gillis, of Upper Margaree, are pipers that would electrify the stoutest hearts in Scotland and the fairest ears as well.

Egypt plenteously abounds in crystal clear fountains. In summer Egypt smiles with strawberries. Smiles enjoyed as far as Upper Margaree by the lovers of good living and by the romantic.

Between Egypt and Gilander's Mountain, Middle River, Victoria County, there is a defile through the forest for three miles duration. Over this road a buggy will roll and jolt with some safety, barring accidents.

Shortly after emerging from the forests, the tourist sights Middle River, upon which he is apt to gaze "long and thoughtfully," as Napoleon Bonaparte gazed on Moscow.

On Gilander's lives Donald A. MacDonald. His is a family whose friendship I will ever treasure. They are pleasant and hospitable and their financial plenitude enables them to attest to their kindness in an enjoyable manner.

From MacDonald's to the river the distance is about three miles. The Presbyterian Church here is a comely building.

Along the road you may telescope landscapes most beautiful and farms that may remind you of those of Ontario.

The river is "a silver thread" that attracts many trout and salmon sports. In its bed gold is found in modest quantities. Deeper search may reveal more of that ever-valued element.

The road soon slopes up Hunter's Mountain (called after Mr. John Hunter), and from the highest degree which the road describes you may behold combinations of scenery and contrasts, about which a Byron might compose a Lochnagar.

By and by you pass through Big Baddeck and over the bridge which is so lofty that you experience cold chills as you go across.

Along to Baddeck town the road is inlaid with spruce trees, hence, is rather monotonous. Four miles travelled and you are in town.

Baddeck is a lovely town. There are many fine houses and several churches. The post-office would be a credit to a city.

Steamboats, etc., without number call at Baddeck.

Across the harbour may be seen the ghost or perhaps the skeleton of the ill fated "May Queen."

Baddeck people are exemplary. They are industrious, artistic and kind. Much and varied work and business is daily done. Money is plentiful. Loungers are few. In politics the voters are practical; decorum prevails.

With due respect to others, about Allan MacDonald, blacksmith. I hold that he and Mrs. MacDonald are individuals whose acquaintance is worth having. Mr. MacDonald is a violinist. Indeed, a visit to Allan Mac-Donald's is something which no one will ever think of without a thrill of joy.

From Baddeck to St. Ann's the miles number ten. The road is good. On the way you pass an I.O.G. T. Lodge.

From Upper Margaree to St. Ann's the people along the road are good, always profuse in furnishing information or any other restorative the wayworn may require.

# Chapter V

# St. Ann's

IN THE EASTERN PART of Victoria County, a few miles to the west of Great Bras d'Or, the tourist suddenly beholds a bay which is truly lovely. This is St. Ann's Bay. It is over six miles in length, and has an average breadth of over a mile.

At the mouth of St. Ann's Bay, on the west side is the town, Englishtown. The people of Englishtown are remarkably progressive. Education receives due attention. In short, the success of Englishtown people is a vivid example of what can be achieved by patient study and continued labor.

Along the bay, for the most part, and on both sides, are excellent farms. The scenic beauty of these cozy farms ranges from the simple to the picturesque. A reasonable number and quantity of north temperature plants are grown. Well blooded horses are plentiful. Cows and calves add a lustre to their allotted villas, while in the lofty distance sturks, oxen, sheep, etc., can be seen in vast numbers.

Scores of sailing and steaming vessels plough the waters of St. Ann's every week. As these gigantic cradles gently rock, they resemble fabulous vultures of the deep in the act of sunning themselves and resting moreover before taking one of their long and happy flights.

There is a sufficiency of wharves. Not far from one of these is a saw-mill which would be no disgrace to a lumber company in New Brunswick. The rapidity of this mill in shingle sawing reminds one of marvelous tales reported about sleight of hand.

The roads are pretty good. Iron bridges appear to be very fashionable, for brooks of very ordinary pretentions

11

babble the "go on forever" boast:—They've bridged me o'er with iron.

The southern end of the main bay is extended by a creek. The neck between this superfluous head and the bay is designated South Gut.

Into the west side of St. Ann's Bay rolls the lordly North River. The river flows through a fertile region. Yes, the farmers of North River need but "tickle the ground, and it smiles with a harvest." Again, North River hay, pressed or otherwise, has more than local reputation.

But, reverting to St. Ann's, the people are agreeable, cheerful and hospitable. Young and old seem to be exceptionally robust. As a rule, the people are good looking. To "treat extensively" upon this might be indiscreet, for two reasons which need not be told.

Three churches, magnificent buildings, emphatically testify to the "applied Christianity" of the place. One of these buildings is elsewhere mentioned. The religion is Presbyterianism.

There are several I. O. G. T. Lodges. The object of those ladies and gentlemen who meet here is to suppress intemperance.

The school sections are large and populous. Good work, and plenty of it, is being done in the schools. The chief occupations of St. Ann's people are farming, fishing, navigating and lumbering. Farming heads the list in lucrative importance, the others follow as above respectively in order of descending magnitude of profit.

In these industries there is gradual but steady improvement. New blood and new capital is occasionally introduced. Equanimity prevails, and it is reasonable to suppose that St. Ann's will yet vie with historic places of eminence.

The homes of St. Ann's might remind the tourist of Mrs. Heman's poetic tribute to the lovely "homes of England." The exteriors of these (the former) are only excelled by their interiors. Clumps of flowery flower-plants are seen in discreet profusion mildly blooming outside the inviting open doors of these palatial cottages, as if the florid sources of varied sweetness within "had run o'er," as the gold of Venice seemed, to Rogers, yes, "had run o'er," which necessitated the removal of the plant inhabitants outside the music resounding walls.

The fisheries off St. Ann's are far-famed. Fishing is quite a significant source of wealth. Formerly however, United States traders came up the bay to purchase bait, and paid a high price therefor. Directly this filled the coffers of St. Ann's men; but indirectly reckoning, 'tis better for St. Ann's, like other parts of the Dominion of Canada, to deal with others in preference to United States people. To-day, and no one regrets it, the United States flag is seldom seen in the bay.

One reason for the collapse of United States trade here was the fact that our laws obliged the Americans to buy licenses ere proceeding to trade with us. This they thought rather oppressive, hence exit, and no one sings, "Will ye no come back again."

Many of St. Ann's young men "take a loup (leap) and o'er the sea." They are smart on the sea and their promotion is usually rapid. They are regularly well paid, and later in life these marines generally settle on a farm or else open a store or a kindred industry.

In winter the forests resound with perpetual reports of the axe. Beech, birch, maple, ash, elm, spruce, fir, hemlock, juniper and pine are here in abundance. In due time the yarded lumber is conveyed to the whistling and everhungry circular saws. Many jolly crowds are engaged in the varied employments which these illusions suggest.

St. Ann's has moreover a plentiful store of gypsum better known as "plaster Paris." This mineral, when thoroughly utilized, will prove its great value in several different phases.

In fact, St. Ann's is a country which no one would desire to leave. A description thereof that would do justice thereto would occupy a volume. True, this country has a few faults and drawbacks, but those weigh but very little against the merits which preponderate overwhelmingly.

The merchants are a fine set of men. They buy and sell fairly, and have discarded the credit system long ago; but liberally assist a customer or a stranger on credit, if it lies in their financial power, when a special emergency justifies the concession.

There are justices of the peace, lawyers and medical doctors. The land is so peaceful and healthful that these men have little or nothing to do; such is St. Ann's.

## Chapter VI

# MacAskill's Appearance, Size, etc.

IN APPEARANCE Angus MacAskill was prepossessing. His eyes and countenance bespoke a stern and shrewd mind tempered with kindness.

His height was seven and three-fourths feet. He was three feet and eight inches across the shoulders. The palm of his hand was six inches wide and twelve inches long. One of his boots at least is still extant, and is eighteen inches long. A coat and vest of his are to be seen in Boston, Mass., and the vest can be comfortably buttoned over two good sized men. Though his face was becomingly plump, he was never fat. Touching on his face it is interesting to know that it was positively beardless. Hence he was never obliged to patronize the consolations of the barber's chair except for a hair cut or a shampoo. His eyes were blue and deep set. His voice, though musical, was somewhat hollow, owing to his massive wind organism. The reader may gain a faint idea of his resonant voice by getting a friend to sit in an empty puncheon and speak. He weighed over 500 pounds. He was affable, courteous and friendly. His hospitality was famous. His character strongly reminded people of Goldsmith's lines in praise of his father. He frequently visited his friends.

Like all good and great men, he had enemies and opponents, but, as he always trod the path of virtue in addition to his strength, his enemies and opponents never got the upper hand literally, financially or pugilistically, or generally speaking in any way. Yet he never risked the extention of his lines by trying too many things.

He was in religion a Presbyterian. At the age of twenty his knowledge of the Bible was extensive. Sundays, or Sabbaths as the reader may choose to call these days of rest and devotion, he carefully observed. A Mr. Campbell, writing from Riverside, California, for the Montreal "Star," says in addition to other information about MacAskill: "He conducted meetings in his own (MacAskill's) house on Sunday." This not only attests to his knowledge of Scripture, it proves that he endeavoured to conform his life to the truths condescended to happy men on the inspired pages.

He seldom went to any church save the one of his own parish, not even to a Presbyterian church, because his presence was liable to draw the attention of the congregation too much. This was his reason. He clearly saw the danger and governed himself accordingly. But this was probably excessive modesty, or modesty a little misdirected. 'Twere better for him to attend.

It may be superfluous to say that he was not a bigot. No, far from it. Though firmly attached to his own religious belief, he treated the expression of different religious opinions with cautious gravity and invariable leniency.

Such, such was Angus MacAskill, a man whose size, strength, kindness, virtues, and exploits will be long remembered. In his own realm of greatness he was the Bonnie

Charlie, the Wallace, the Bruce, the Napoleon Bonaparte, the Marshall Ney, the Wellington, the Nelson, the O'Connell, the Robert Burns or the Washington of his countless friends, according as they happened to be impressed by the different phases of his greatness.

Even to-day in Cape Breton, and in many another land, the mere mention of St. Ann's Big Boy creates a sensation. But while we rejoice at the greatness of our hero, let us not forget the unremitting loyalty of Cape Breton to her sons and daughters. She never "warps or swerves or stirs" from what she thought or spoke of them, and when they leave her like wanton birds, who paint aloft upon her flag the modest welcome, come what may:—"Will ye na come back again."

Yes, hundreds of eminent people yearly vie with one another in sounding the praises of the Cape Bretonians. It is gratifying to reflect upon the fact that our reputation is often the subject of friendly discussions within the "merry homes of England."

These remarks, far from deducting from our hero's claim to what we call immortal fame, make his claim so much the stronger, for such a people would not care to "throw up their bonnets" for one not highly worthy of such an inestimable tribute.

## Chapter VII

# MacAskill's Ancestors

AT THIS STAGE of our hero's life and exploits, it is both reasonable and natural that the reader will be curious to know something of his ancestors. Were there any giants among them? It has been said already that his father was but of moderate size, and that his mother was a good size woman. But the reader before proceeding with this phase, a few remarks on heredity may not be inappropriate.

Nature works in mysterious ways. A child may bear a striking facial resemblance to his father, while his limbs may resemble those of his maternal grandfather. Again a man may not be the picture of his paternal grandfather. But in the case of such a man the points of resemblance were there, though not evinced. Moreover, a man may be found to be almost a duplicate of a great grand uncle. Yet, as a rule, and as a rule a salutary thing it is, children are ideal images of their parents. And though "Auld Nature" wantonly as if by accident deviates occasionally from her rule far enough to use anew the mould in which our remote ancestors were moulded, it rather strengthens than weakens the belief that Nature intended us all to be and to look a little or more like one another, and like Adam and Eve. This phenomenon of Nature is called heredity.

In our hero's paternal ancestral line, if we go back several generations, yes, several centuries, we will find another giant (a MacAskill) whose prowess was almost equally great. With said exception, our hero's ancestry were people of average size.

Now it is possible that that MacAskill line may yet startle the world by producing another herculean specimen of humanity.

But in the case of our hero, Angus MacAskill, climatic influences the most favorable, as elsewhere suggested, and other circumstances possibly were powerful auxiliaries of Nature in building his stupendous body and in its thorough development.

It may be remarked that as a baby he was so small that no one expected him to live. As time passed he began to grow, and grow in earnest.

After the age of eight years until he arrived at maturity he always ate a bowl of palatable mixture of cream and oatmeal, sometimes called crowdie, after each meal. Such a desert might seem crude and unattractive to some, yet it was good and mention thereof may serve to show the wisdom of substantial diet; it slams the door on the dwarf's nose in the days of growth.

How sweet to see our hero, doffing his bonnet to enjoy his modest but superb repast. And who would dare to scoff?

## Chapter VIII

# MacAskill Used Tobacco

THOSE WHO DO NOT USE TOBACCO cannot be blamed though they condemn the tobacco habit. Of course there are some who do not touch tobacco, who care little or nothing whether others smoke, chew, snuff or not. Others are readily sickened by tobacco fumes. To these, passing swiftly through a smoking car is an ordeal which they would not like to repeat. This respect is one of the many in which variations of or differing constitutions are expressed. What is one man's medicine is another man's poison, though not a well underpinned principle bears the winds of time fairly well, and the researches made by the moderns reveal that it will rock there yet for quite a while.

The above mentioned maxim (did I say principle?) has been well illustrated in one of the foreign regions somewhat. A certain lad, a soldier, decided to try his fortunes as a doctor. He did not go to college or to a university, but just bought a valise of medicine and a few implements. He has R.R.R., G.G.G. Hood's Sarsparilla, Ayer's Cherry Pectoral etc. Thus equipped he joined another division of the army and enlisted as a doctor. His first patient was a Dutchman down with a raging fever. Give me "sour kraut" shouted the poor Dutchman. The doctor (so-called) got his patient the cabbage soup. The dutchman swallowed his fill, and soon recovered. The doctor wrote in his professional diary. "Sour kraut cures fever." Next morning he was called to attend a Prussian, who was all but gone with the fever. The doctor gave him sour kraut, and in five minutes the Prussian was dead. The aristocratic Prussian constitution was ruined by sour kraut. The doctor wrote in his diary as follows: — Sour kraut heals a Dutchman's fever, but it is a Prussian's coup de grace (or finishing stroke).

Now a medicine, drug, or even a narcotic, may suit one person better than his twin brother. Some who receive a charge of either never recover in perfection. There are others who experience no evil consequences.

But is tobacco a failure? Thousands answer "Yes" and hundreds answer "no." That tobacco users are in the minority is no argument against its use. Medical knowledge or science cautiously advises the world to avoid tobacco. Said science teaches that a moderate dose of smoke or an occasional chew or a frequent shot of snuff has no ill consequences of a very material nature. But here, as in many other things, people are in danger of overstepping moderation, and, moreover, tobacco, like strong drink, usually causes a greater appetite for what? for more of itself. If too much tobacco be taken, it impairs or injures the mind and the body, makes a person bad looking, clumsy and weak. If you once begin, it is, you may say, impossible to discontinue the tobacco habit. In fighting with your inclinations, you are but one against two. First, force of habit is against you; secondly, you have the insidious craving for the weed, which is a more bitter enemy than the first. Don't begin to use tobacco; no, don't touch it if you mean to stop using it some other day. It is a pungent, that is, a bad smelling weed, too, as it does no good; that is, as it is usually taken, why not leave it alone? Of course, applied to cuts or snake bites, etc., it is a valuable medicine.

However, it is well to make known that our hero used tobacco. He was "barely yet past his teens" when he acquired the habit. In those times, smoking was somewhat fashionable, and, of course, MacAskill could afford to smoke as well as his mates.

One of his pipes is still extant, and it is a marvel of size. It is cherry wood, one of the limbs serving the function of stem. Possibly it was made on a colossal scale merely for merriment, not for the sake of logical proportion. It will hold one-sixth of a pound of tobacco at a time, and resembles a mallet in the distance.

But to be serious, tobacco had no ill effects on MacAskill's body. He was so robust and able that it would take tobacco half a century to make the least impression on him. Should his supply get exhausted he did not care very much, for he could control his craving till it was convenient to have his orders sent.

### Chapter IX

# MacAskill Would Take A Glass

THE FOLLY OF DRINKING intoxicating liquors has been often and conclusively proved. The arguments advanced in favor of strong drink are very shadowy. But against strong drink score of able arguments can be adduced, and this without great study or research. At this day no self-respecting person bothers with tangle-foot at all.

But in former years, say, thirty or forty years ago, it

was not known that alcoholic liquors were so pernicious. It remained for the present studious, laborious and researching generations to discover the danger. Rum, etc., injures a person morally, physically, mentally and financially. This being admitted, why would anyone drink strong drink? The author of this book ventures to answer that question. It is because rum, etc., so to speak, creates cheerfulness and happiness.

But, dear reader, this cheerfulness and this happiness are merely counterfeits, yes, merely delusions. One smile is more beneficial to a sober person than a peal of laughter to the man who is "pretty full." Again, after the direct effects of a glass or more of rum, etc., are over, there is a reaction. The man is dull and sad—there are penalties which he must pay for the folly of drinking alcoholic drinks. Really now, there is no pleasure in rum, etc., drinking; it does not heat you in cold weather, except in your imagination; hence, I ask again, why drink the hateful liquor at all?

But, as already suggested, some years ago the evil resultants of alcoholic drinks had not been discovered. This serves as an ample apology for those who drank them. No further apology is needed for anyone. Another helping or auxiliary apology is the fact that the intoxicating drinks for sale then were not adulterated. They were not additionally poisoned with soda, tobacco, etc., etc.

Angus MacAskill took a glass of rum, brandy or whiskey occasionally. Did I say glass? Well, twas a mistake. He used to drink out of a wooden dish called a tub. The tub would hold three glasses. However, ordinarily speaking, strong drink did not hurt Angus MacAskill, i.e., to any apparent extent. He was so healthy and strong that a few drinks a week did not injure him.

No one will dream of disrespecting the memory of Angus MacAskill on account of the knowledge that he drank strong liquors. No! No! Drinking was customary in his day, and as aforesaid it was supposed to be harmless. In fact, drinking was thought to be a semi-elixir which would make perfect health better and cure every ailment peculiar to the age.

About rum, etc.—our hero was no niggard in a liquor store. He'd call for a drink for all hands soon as he'd enter, no matter whether the crowd was large or small.

He did not sell strong liquor himself, but often had some in his store for private use. Any customer whom he knew to be fond of the "drop," would get a hearty swallow, and then in the din of funny yarns broken only by laughter, he'd drink a "shot" himself.

Had our hero been of the present day, we may be sure that he'd be an advocate of total abstinence. However, be it said that drinking never excited him to any visible extent, and that he never drank to intoxication.

## Chapter X

# MacAskill Could Farm

IN HIS EARLY YEARS, except fishing, no work pleased our hero more than farming. He could plough, harrow, and in short, was an adept at all those duties peculiar to the farm. He was an expert plowman. This is interesting to the farmer reader, for he knows that ploughing is one thing and ploughing admirably well another. Our hero became versed in the science and art of ploughing at a very early age. He was carefully trained to it by his father, who always tried to have the following momentous principle practically applied:—What's worth doing at all is worth doing well.

His father taught him the wisdom of having one general principle in all doings instead of trying to follow many rules. His father often demonstrated that, if men do their duty to the best of their judgment, power and strength, it matters little whether the motives are selfish or not. He showed that there is no antagonism between doings that are really good; in fine, that what is really and positively good is good and cannot be bad: yes, that what is good for one man is good for all, directly or indirectly. Moreover, he held that nothing approximates the expression of the above principle as near as the golden rule, to wit: "Do to others as you would have others do to you." Such was the philosophic general instruction imparted to our hero, to which he largely owed "that prudent, cautious self control which is wisdom's root." Wonder not that the son of such a parent was morally and generally a whole man.

He loved his mother too deep and too much for words. Nothing pained him so much as to see her sad. He spared no pains for her comfort. Her word was law to him, and he never persisted in anything of which she disapproved.

One instance will serve to prove this quite emphatically. He and his father were out ploughing one afternoon. A neighbor came around, and in the course of a colloquy with our hero, bet ten dollars that the field would not be finished that evening. Our hero put up ten dollars, too, and the neighbor went off till a later hour. Soon, however, one of the horses got sick, and had to be unyoked for that day, whereupon MacAskill stepped into the horse's place, took hold of the traces, and was fairly more than a match for the remaining horse. He filled the sick horse's place successfully for two hours.

At four o'clock his mother came out with a luncheon. She was astounded. In fact she wept. She prayed her son to cease such work at once, and never to do the like again. Without a word of explanation our hero begged her pardon, which was readily granted.

Luncheon over, he walked home and smoked for a while. Then he pocketed ten dollars out of his safe, and paid the bet. Were it not for his mother's interference, he would have won the bet, but rather than hurt his mother's feelings he let his money go.

'Twas months afterwards that his mother heard of the wager. She was sorry, yet she was satisfied that she did right to interpose. The good lady was right, for,

A pebble on the streamlet scant
Has turned the course of many a river:
A dewdrop on the plant
Has warped the giant oak forever.

Hence her interposing probably stayed him for these happy years at least from indiscreet undertakings which might end disastrously. "A man's a man for all that," no matter how great his strength, and labours usually assigned to engines or beasts of burden are too heavy for the strongest man, at least if continued, and moreover a little undignifying.

Years afterwards he said: my mother's counsel on that occasion cost me ten dollars, but to me it was worth a thousand.

Let all mothers who read this endeavour to train their sons to refrain from indiscreet undertakings. Thus, they'll confer a favour on all humanity, for in a great measure, as Napoleon Bonaparte said, "the cradle rules the world."

## Chapter XI

# He Surprises His Father

WHEN ALL THE WORLD is young, lad,
And all the trees are green;
And every goose a swan, lad,

24

And every lass a queen;
Then hey for boot and horse, lad,
And around the world away,—
Young blood must have its course, lad,
And every man his day.

Though by no means a vain-minded person, our hero's chief pastime, in his early days, was the performing of feats which might startle veteran circus spectators. But in his case the feats were real, and devoid of all trickery, jugglery and sleight of hand.

He was a giant by nature. He never attended a gymnasium. We can barely imagine the result had science and art been brought to bear on the developing of his strength.

At the age of fourteen he was known as St. Ann's Big Boy. He moved slowly, and had nothing to do with other boys of the same age as long as he had more mature company. This was not owing to precocity, but because these contemporaries of his, possibly through jealousy, were wont to tease him about his size and his slowly gait. When, however, our hero showed signs of anger, they took to their heels.

As above intimated, he was not precocious. At this age, though big, his mind was boyish. He enjoyed his own innocent sports with as much zest as other youths enjoyed theirs.

Touching on precocity in children and young people, nothing is more ridiculous. It is invariably the fault of the parents, guardians and teachers. Those who instruct children and young people surely ought to know that, if it were better for the young to think and act like mature people, that they would be instinctively inclined to do so, and competent, too, of themselves alone. Parents and others cannot give laws to Nature, but they should carefully co-operate with Nature. They should allow children to indulge in childish pastimes. In fact, parents, guardians and teachers ought to encourage in those under their jurisdiction such studies, plays and labours as are only suitable for the young. The great majority of the world's celebrated women and men did not think or act like grown up people until they passed their teens.

Reason, common sense and history combine to prove that precocity is a great danger, or, at best, an utter failure, for it places the youth in the embarrassing situation of the "daw in borrowed feathers."

About the first time he showed his great strength was when he was sixteen. In those pioneer days boards were sawn by the whip-saw; the logs were placed on what was called a pit seven or eight feet from the ground, and it took a good deal of strength to put up the logs. Our hero and his father were one day sawing boards in this primitive way. For once in their lives, the two disagreed about something. The dinner conch sounded as they had just got a heavy log on to the pit. His father went to dinner, but our hero did not go. When his father returned, the log was laying on the ground, whereupon he accused his son of gathering neighbors to help him in doing mischief. Our hero then seized the log and threw it up on the pit as if it were a little block.

He then said to his father, "We have quarrelled a little, but I am sorry. As it was our first quarrel, let it be our last. But in a manner I am glad that it was you, for, if it were many a man, the possibilities are that I'd relieve him of his head with one clip of my hand." He extended his hand to his father. They shook hands in silence, and they never had a cross word again.

Indeed, he loved his parents dearly. Filial love, yes, exceptional filial love, always merits admiration. Most great men of ancient and modern times loved their parents or their guardians, as the case might be, to a degree almost incredible. Angus MacAskill was not an exception. Nothing that he could do for his parents comfort or welfare was left undone, and woe to him whether friend or foe who would insult them when he was near. In this he has left the young people an example by which they can benefit, and, as one laudable thought or deed breeds another, and so on, that example may be the means whereby some may rise step by step to a position where they can take advantage of "that tide in the affairs of men which taken at the flood leads on to fortune."

## Chapter XII

# He Loses a Friend, But No Enmity

SOME OF THE EXPLOITS of Angus MacAskill, like those of some of the celebrities in other walks of life, savour of the curious; one of these is sufficient. Were many of these given, the author would possibly suffer the odium of being classed among the liars of the age. However, none of these reflect a ray on our hero which would lead one to suspect him of want of sense or of virtue.

Here is a word picture of the exploit suggested:

One day our hero and a friend of his set off afoot on a journey of thirty miles or so. They arrived at their destination, and, having discharged their errand, they resolved to return home that evening. They directed their steps homeward, and all "went merry as a marriage bell" till about dusk, when a tempestuous thunder storm rolled along.

"And such a night they take the road in
As ne'er poor mortal was abroad in."

Down poured the rain. MacAskill viewed the excited elements with composure.

But for the rain he would have been delighted, for he had a keen relish to the awful and sublime. He asked his friend if he would like to call anywhere. His friend said that he would rather go home. "All right," said MacAskill, "but I see you are getting tired, come on my back, I'll carry you."

His friend laughed an objection, but our hero insisted. So after a few moments our hero was walking swiftly along with his friend perched on his back.

The lightning flashed, the electric bolts shot zigzag where something was scented to devour, the thunder rolled; but MacAskill was not alarmed. He told his funniest yarns.

When within a mile of home his friend remarked that he had recently heard that a friend of theirs was sick in Texas, adding that enquires ought to be made whether he was out of money, etc.

MacAskill was touched. He became silent at once. Absorbed by the sad news, he unconsciously let his friend slip off his back. His friend said nothing, but walked on behind.

Not until our hero had got home did he think of his burden. His friend, though weighing one hundred and ninety pounds, was in the matter of weight so trifling to him that his back never missed him.

His friend soon arrived, and after both had a sumptuous repast, they went to bed, and were up again hale and hearty in "the morning early."

The round trip, sixty miles, was quite a distance to walk, but our hero did not mind it. Had he a distant errand to perform the next day he would gladly go. He was so strong, and his step so long, that a hundred miles a day would not cause him serious fatigue.

## Chapter XIII

# He Shakes Hands in Dead Earnest

NOW—here's a hand, my trusty friend,
And gie's a hand of thine,
And we'll take a cup of kindness yet
For old lang syne.

One day at the time when MacAskill's fame was dawning, a renowned figure put in his appearance. MacAskill soon suspected something, but made no remarks. He entertained the stranger in true Cape Breton style. This reminds one of Roderick Dhu's attitude towards his illustrious guest, James V. of Scotland, when they met in wilds of that "home of the happy." At length the question arose, is this burly stranger going to perpetrate a miniature Glencoe massacre in St. Ann's? At length the suspicious case requested our hero to fight him. MacAskill remonstrated with him, told him that pugilism was an abomination, and fraught with evils many. But the stranger persisted, and charged our hero with cowardice. The latter at last said, "All right, my friend, but let us shake hands." Well, dear reader, they did shake hands. MacAskill squeezed the unfortunate man's hand, which caused the blood to flow freely through the tips of the latter's fingers. This stranger was, of course, more fortunate than Sir Henry de Bohun who tried to assassinate King Robert Bruce at Bannockburn. Yet, it is probable that he never thought of his adventure with MacAskill without a sense of shame and fear. However, he retreated hastily from St. Ann's, well convinced as Britannia rules the waves, Cape Breton rules the earth in the realm of muscular strength.

Not long after this event, another man came to see

MacAskill; nay, not only to see him, but to wrestle with him. As before, our hero was loath to wrestle or to open hostilities for fame or curiosity. His mighty heart was brimful of charitable humanity. He invariably held that men ought not to wrestle, fight and such like without plausible reasons. He recognized the principle which Burns thus set before us:

"Then gently scan your brother man,
Still gentlier sister woman;
Although they go a trifle wrong,
To step aside is human.
One point must still be greatly dark,
The moving why they do it;
And just as lamely can you mark
How far perhaps they rue it.
Who made the heart, 'tis He alone
Decidedly can try us;
He knows each chord, its various tone,
Each spring—its various bias;
Then at the balance let's be mute,
We never can adjust it;
What's done we partly may compute.
But know not what's resisted."

But when he saw the impossibility of convincing his would-be antagonist of the barbarity of wanton wrestling, fighting, etc., he got hold of him. Near by there was a woodpile fully ten feet in height and twenty feet in width on top. As already said, MacAskill got hold of the man and threw him over the woodpile. Yes, though he weighed over three hundred pounds, he was sent whistling over that woodpile, describing a curve like a projectile fired from a mortar.

This stranger was a United States sea-captain. Some of his crew met him on the beach on his departure from MacAskill's. Their boat required some ballast, and they proceeded to take stones and rocks, therefore off MacAskill's farm. Our hero said nothing till they were through. Thereupon, he lit his pipe and strode leisurely down to the shore. The boat was put to sea, and had moved out above one hundred feet when our hero got to the shore. "Say, captain," said MacAskill, "get back here with those stones and rocks you took."

"What do you want them for?" said the captain. "It matters not," said MacAskill, "but it was a dirty mean trick to take them under the circumstances without my permission."

"I will not send them back," responded the captain, "but if you go out again to my vessel, you will stand a show to get them."

MacAskill seized a stone and threw it at the boat. The one stone damaged the boat so much that the captain judged it was better to surrender in time.

The boat rowed back and the captain and his men were obliged to put each stone and rock exactly where it was before, while our hero superintended the work with a beaming countenance which showed the appreciating by-standing boys of St. Ann's how highly he was amused with the captain's humiliation.

"The sun had now gone out of sight
Behind the mountains tall;
And on the same around his feet
The dew began to fall."
—Malcolm H. Gillis

And now the ballast episode being over, MacAskill walked home, meditating with wonder on the vanities and follies of some men. His home that night was crammed with eager visitors who came to congratulate him. Soon the sound of choice music from violin and bag-pipe rose over the sweet and delicious music of happy voices. "Eyes spake love to eyes that spake again." The dance begins. The celebration was a success and a delightful one.

Such were the early days of MacAskill. Such were his exploits. How pleasant to reflect on the fact that as an exceptional man, he was timely recognized and appreciated. His recognition and appreciation by his friends and countrymen was to him an ample reward for wisely using his muscular superiority. Of him it cannot be said:

> "He who is truly wise or great
> Lives both too early or too late."

## Chapter XIV

# He Goes to a Frame-Raising

THEN LET US PRAY that come it may,
And come it will for all that;
That man to man the world o'er
Shall brothers be and all that. —Burns

The Cape-Bretonians are far-famed for their unanimity, and for the strict observance of the Golden Rule. If a Cape Bretonian happens to need assistance of any kind, he has only to undergo the ordeal of making his wants known.

Their unanimity has proved a general blessing. The merits of unanimity were well illustrated once by an old man. He was contemplating the matter of embarkation to eternity which was "too, too soon" to be inevitable, and before leaving he desired to give his family an object lesson, the last of many, which would crown all the rest. He got a few sticks, put them together, side by side, and tried to break them across the knee. Having failed he took the sticks separately and broke them easily.

"Now, my dears," he said, "there is strength in union, and if you practice unanimity you shall be much more apt to succeed." Shortly after he died. His family observed his counsel and the result was that they became the leading men of the place, "with wealth at their will."

The absence of unanimity has retarded the progress of nations. It has something to do with the failure of Charles Edward Stuart (Bonny Price Charles). Yes, dissensions retarded the progress of Scotland, Ireland and England. Even in our great Dominion of Canada, dissensions, political and otherwise, have sometimes proved very embarrassing.

Not so in the island of Cape Breton. What dissensions we have had owed their origin to varied opinions respecting the means to be employed for certain praiseworthy ends. As all parties were sincere, and meant to do good, and did good, these superficial tempests were almost essential constituents of unanimity.

A discreet quantity of word warring strengthens the right. The difficulty is to gauge ourselves at the proper time. The philosophy of the benefits of opposition suggested in the preceding sentence is something that only one in two thousand have learned.

Those who have not time to study large books on this philosophy can proceed in anther way. Let them watch and observe discussions. As a rule they will find that the results of discussions where all thought and spoke alike are always weak.

But to our hero. A neighbor of his was to have a barn frame raising on a certain day. As customary in such cases, he requested his neighbors to "give him a lift." The call was promptly and cheerfully responded to by the arrival of sixty or seventy men, Angus MacAskill among the rest like a lighthouse among lamp-posts.

The frame was not quite ready, and MacAskill peeled off and went to work with the big augur. As he worked he noticed that the crowd were getting "unco happy," and the breath of the first man that came in close proximity to him reminded him of a rum distillery. That was enough. He understood that for some reason he was to be neglected that day by the frame owner. He said nothing. He was not very fond of strong drink anyway, but he was none the less insulted at heart.

The frame was raised, and ready for the rafters when the dinner bell rang. MacAskill loitered behind, and when the rest had entered the house he went to the frame, climbed up, and lowered one of the side plaits, a stick 60 ft. x 8 in., put it on his shoulder, and walked off with it. He made for the sea-shore, which was about four hundred yards away, and consigned the plait to the Atlantic Ocean.

The splash was heard in the house, but they dared not go to ask for explanations. Our hero walked away satisfied in leaving a token of his displeasure.

On his way home he called at a certain grocery store. He asked for a pound of tea. The proprietor said: "Well, Mr. MacAskill, take a handful out of that box, and if it weighs one half of one pound, I'll charge you nothing." MacAskill tried as requested. The handful was weighed, and it weighed one pound. The merchant offered him a whole box as a present, but this was politely refused, and went home.

## Chapter XV

# He Was Not Vain

AS ALREADY OBSERVED, it was the good fortune of our hero that he was not swayed over much by vanity. Of course, he duly appreciated the praise of his admirers but not to excess. On the contrary this power of the mind is essential in the mental organism. But, like the other faculties, it requires Providential grace for its suitable enlivenment and a grace-pervaded reason or understanding for its guidance and moderation. Given these akin to essential requisites, vanity is a treasure.

Some of the greatest men had a seasonable dash of vanity. Where is the young man that would not face astounding odds for the sweet encomiums his darling can bestow upon him? Where is a man, young or old, who would not fight and die for his country with joy, if he were confident that his name would be placed on the list of heroes, to be honoured for all time. They have not been born—at least in Cape Breton Island.

However, as already intimated, MacAskill was not a slave to vanity, nor to any other passion. But by the way, it is gratifying to know that his great size, and strength, by no means a brake on his contentment. He took as lively an interest in himself, as a natural prodigy, as others took. It is said that "it is a wise boy that knows his own father." Very good, but wiser still is he who knows himself. MacAskill wisely endeavored, discreetly, of course, to gain an idea of his own exceptional value, so to speak, but in the line of strength he failed, because he never failed, for he never attempted a lift or kindred feat without succeeding with wonderful ease.

From the above gleanings the reader, at least after some reflection, can realize the utility of vanity. Harmonizing with the other faculties of the mind, as in the case of our hero, vanity in one sense ceases to be vanity, yet constitutes a whip whose strength or weakness influences man to a high degree.

Our hero often merited and enjoyed the applause of ladies and gentlemen by passing swiftly over the sidewalk with two barrels of salted pork, one under each arm. In getting the barrels under his arms he did not experience much difficulty.

Lifting a hundred weight with two fingers, and raising it till his arm arrived at a horizontal pose, was mere child's play to him. But who else could do that? Reader think well. Add to this that he could hold his arm in that position for ten minutes. Even this will convey the idea of his superior strength to permanent conviction.

But not to lower the fame of MacAskill, but to solidify it by fair comparison, it may be said that two Cape Bretonians, a Neil MacDonald, of West Ainslie, and a John MacFarlane, of Upper Margaree (both of them untrained), did something tough too. The former took a weight of 86 lbs. on his little finger and wrote his name legibly at a level with his face. The latter wrote his name at the same height with a 56-pounder suspended from his little finger. These men were but common sized, and did well. But be it said that great as MacAskill's size was, his strength was greater in proportion to his size than that displayed in the above comparison.

## Chapter XVI

# MacAskill Helps a Friend

COURAGE BROTHER! do not stumble,
Though thy path be dark as night
There's a star to guide the humble;
Trust in God and do the right.

The hero of this history was uncommonly warm-hearted. The poor and oppressed of his day never appealed to him in vain.

It is a happy fact that the great majority of the world's great women and great men have been in all ages exceptionally charitable and devoid of unreasonable pride and haughtiness. This is worthy of young people's earnest consideration. However, an instance or two will serve to illustrate the truth of what has been above asserted of his warm-heartedness.

Once upon a time, a certain man, humble in circumstances, presented himself at a certain store and asked the proprietor, an acquaintance of his, to let him have a barrel of flour on credit. Times were dull and hence the merchant was the same. He gave the poor would-be purchaser a look of merchantable contempt which meant a positive refusal, but said nothing. Again and again the man made known the object of his call, and told the merchant that his wife and little children were on the verge of starvation. Again and again no answer, save the whistling of the simple and mellow music of "Home, sweet home."

"I have a vessel down here at the wharf. There are several barrels of flour in the hold. If you throw the barrel out of the hold on deck, a height of twelve feet, the barrel is yours," and warming up with excitement, he added: "Yes, you can have all the barrels that you or any man can throw on deck."

"That's pretty tall talking," said the poor man, "there are lots of strong men in the world."

The merchant was nettled a little bit by the man's sober reply and said, "I defy you to procure a man in St. Ann's that can do what I have proposed."

The man shrugged his shoulders, thought of MacAskill, and proceeded homeward.

His horse was slow, the road bad, and the entire world looked gloomy. The future "was ominous and dark." The man, not withstanding the jolting of the cart, thought of many things. He dreamt of his early days "when his bosom was young." Then he thought of his courtship of the loveliest of them all, and of the many imposing castles he had built in the air before and after marriage. Having come in sight of his home, he espied his wife. He paused, shuddered and wept.

But who happened to come to where he was but

MacAskill. He gleaned from the man's woeful countenance that something was wrong. He asked what was the matter. On being told, he said, "Is your horse tired?" The man said, "No." "Well," said our hero, "let's go back, the distance is not very great."

And off they went. Arrived at the store, our hero walked in and told the merchant that he was ready to purchase flour on the "latest" terms proposed. "All right," sang the merchant.

MacAskill and his friend, accompanied by the merchant, proceeded to the vessel. On the wharf there chanced to be a crowd. Each and all of them were eye witnesses to what occurred.

Our hero jumped on board and down into the hold. It then occurred to his cloudless mind that should he throw some barrels on deck they would be smashed. But resolved not to be outdone, he seized a barrel, threw it. Up through the hatchway it went, and out splashed into the harbour. Out came another, and another until six were floating. Fortunately none of the barrels collided. Thereupon he helped his friend in removing the barrels to the cart and the two set off for their respective homes.

However, be it said that MacAskill was warmly thanked by his friend, and applauded by all the bystanders, the merchant included.

Little by little his friend whom he had so practically helped and indirectly encouraged, improved in the science and art of success. Twelve years afterwards he was quite well to do. Before his death he had several hundred dollars in the bank, and his descendants to day are reputedly among the higher rural class, socially and financially.

## Chapter XVII

# MacAskill Likes Fishing

FISH AND FISHING; where are the eyes that do not sparkle at the mere mentioning of these two musical words. How many happy recollections "flow gently" into the memory. Fish and fishing, "go where you will on land or on sea," these suggestive words, in whatever language spoken, awaken thoughts which never fail to benefit the mind if not your general worldly interests.

Fish and fishing illustrate or illustrate more and better morals than Aesop's fables. The credulity of some fishes, shows the folly of extreme credulity. The imperative painstaking of the fishermen proves the necessity of taking pains in what is to be done before success may be expected. If the reader be a keen observer and thinker, and a person of force, he or she may derive pleasure, recreation and benefit, from a thorough consideration of fish and fishing. But a warning note may not be amiss. It is dangerous to think too much on such matters—half an hour in the afternoon is sufficient.

River fishing or angling is very attractive. It is particularly so to veteran anglers. The new beginners' occasional plights are lovely described by the great author, Washington Irving. Irving humorously remarked that he hooked himself instead of fish, etc., etc., and his comments are so true to life that a person almost fancies that Irving and his associates are all present, well equipped, and, moreover, in imagination, you can almost hear the river of his angling experiences thundering by.

But the accustomed angler's success is an effectual balm for the troubles occasioned by the obstacles he or she needs to surmount. And again a veteran eludes many stumbling blocks.

It may be here remarked that among the best anglers

of Cape Breton Island, the following gentlemen are classed:

Angus J. MacFarlane, Upper Margaree; Dan Hugh MacFarlane, Upper Margaree; Kenneth P. MacKay, Rear, Scotsville; John P. MacKay, Rear, Scotsville; Donald B. Gillis (carpenter) Upper Margaree; John MacLellan (John's son), S. W. Margaree; Alex MacDougall (Archd's son), S. W. Margaree.

The second named one is generally reputed to be a prodigy in the science and art. He is not over fifteen, but was trained by his father, first above mentioned.

Angling is generally pursued for pastime, but salt sea fishing for satisfying hunger and for profit. Sea fishing is vastly important. Millions depend on it, and thousands fish who hate the work, in a manner, but like in other respects because it is the most beneficial industry that lies within reach of their grasp.

Angus MacAskill's favorite amusement and employment was sea-fishing. During the entire fishing season, save when there was a rush of farm work, the dawn of morning opened her beaming eyes to see him in his boat. Early rising, as a rule, is advisable in all walks of life, and it is very necessary for the fisherfolk. It is not necessary to name the principal reasons, for, if you fish, you will soon find out these reasons for yourself, and if you don't fish, you need not be very concerned therewith.

But MacAskill was an exceptionally early riser—first out of bed, and usually the first to go to bed. He took his dinner with him in a satchel; and sometimes a newspaper, book or scribbling book to while away his leisure moments.

He always hated a second-hand or wrecked boat. All the boats he ever had were good ones and large. He usually manned his boat alone, sitting on the stern thwart, of course, rudder in hand.

Before the mast was placed a ballast, a precaution which the weight of our hero seated at the rear rendered essential. Only for this ballast the boat would turn a quarter of a somersault, which would make things rather un-comfortable.

Things that were bettered by painting he made a point of keeping painted. So his boat was not neglected in this respect.

In fact, St. Ann's has seldom, if ever, seen a better fisherman than MacAskill. He cleared a crisp handful of ten dollar bills every year.

When the season was over, he would cart the boat and all his fishing gear to a house expressly built for the purpose. Then he would take up some other work until the "airy wheels of time" a few month's course "had driven."

## Chapter XVIII

# The Fishing Boat Exploit

THE FISHING BOAT EXPLOIT of our hero is a household tale in St. Ann's. But there are either two versions of the same exploit, or there are two sister exploits. For that matter, it differs nothing, as one thing is certain, viz., "something was attempted, something was done," and that something was prodigious in the extreme. The two versions are here subjoined, the former was related to the author by John A. Morrison of South Gut, St. Ann's.

Our hero's favorite pursuit was fishing. One day he was alone in and about his boat. In the evening as he came to the shore, he helloed to the other fishermen to come and help him in with his boat. They soon arrived. One of them secretly proposed that they should push and haul the boat over a hill into a neighboring pool, and leave MacAskill to get it out of there at his leisure. The crowd was a large one, and sure of success. No one breathed the secret to MacAskill. They seized the boat, and up it goes. MacAskill walks by the shoulder of the boat pulling reasonably strong. When the boat arrived at high water mark, MacAskill said, "That will do, thank you." They pretended not to hear him, and up the boat goes, but not very far; MacAskill perceived the trick at a flash, and placed his shoulder to that of the boat. Crack, crack, crack, and the boat is torn apart.

The crowd fled, but our hero grabbed one, and threw him disdainfully up in the air, where he described an arch or semi-circle, landing twenty feet away, more dead than alive with fear and pain.

The second version, or sister exploit (as the case may be), words substantially as follows:

One lovely twilight, our hero and his friends had just come ashore. In their fishing fleet was one boat of the extra weight. The hauling thereof to a safe altitude defied a crowd of brawny veterans. MacAskill was requested to help. Up he came and caught hold. His companions just for fun hauled back with all their strength; MacAskill soon noticed the joke, and decided to have a joke of his own. He gave a ponderous pull, the boat was torn in two from stern to prow.

He carried his half as far as he pleased, and threw it aside. His companions were dumfounded with astonishment. The owner of the boat was quite satisfied. He said that he preferred seeing that exploit than the best boat that ever graced the smiling waters of St. Ann's.

It is said that thereafter St. Ann's men who were given to jokes, tricks, and such like carefully avoided experimenting on Angus MacAskill. On this, and on other occasions, had he been very ill-natured, there had been a tragedy. What would have an ordinary citizen been in his vice-like grasp?

The boat exploit would be a very choice subject for a poem. Possibly the day will arrive when one of our poets will weave a wreath of poetry about that boat, a large, lettered wreath so worded as to spell the immortal name, Angus MacAskill.

## Chapter XIX

# MacAskill Goes to the United States

MR. C.H. CAMPBELL, of Riverside, California, is right when he says in the "Family Herald" and "Weekly Star" and "People's Popular Magazine," as follows in the next paragraph:

A man from New York visited Cape Breton in 1849, and, meeting Angus MacAskill, asked him to go with him, which he consented to do. He engaged him for five years, and they travelled through Canada, the United States, and part of Europe.

He was now twenty-four years of age. After a thorough preparation for his travels, and for his absence from home, he proceeded to bid his friends "a sad and heart-warm fond adieu." He was deeply affected, but could not restrain his surprise at the genuine sorrow manifested by one and all. Not till now did he dream that he was exceptionally beloved. A large crowd escorted him to the shore, where a boat was waiting to convey him and the New Yorker to the vessel. After further leave-taking, his comrades sadly directed their steps homeward. That was a sad evening with them. That was a sad evening at St. Ann's.

The late poet, Alfred Tennyson, has aptly and wisely said:

"I hold it true whate'er befall:
I feel it when I sorrow most:

43

Tis better to have loved and lost
Than never to have loved at all."

Nevertheless parting with one we love is very trying. It is exceptionally hard to bear. Sorrow for absent loved ones has sometimes caused death. It may be proper here to remark in all sincerity that the best thing to do in time of sorrow, ordinarily speaking, is to go to work and to work hard. This antidote or cure does not involve the least disrespect of those whose absence we regret.

Acting on this or a similar maxim of equanimity, our hero's friends soon busied themselves with their usual employments. Before long the welcomed letter arrived from MacAskill. Here is a facsimile thereof:

*Quebec, P.Q., 8ᵗʰ July, 1849*

*Dear Brother: I arrived here safely. The voyage was rather rough, but no accidents occurred. What I have seen of Quebec excels my expectations.*

*I was rather lonely during the passage, though I had a plentitude of suitable and congenial company.*

*My friend, the New York man, is very agreeable. But, notwithstanding, I often reflect o'er the memory of the days which I passed with my friends of bonnie St. Ann's.*

*"Scenes of woe and scenes of pleasure;*
*Scenes that former thoughts renew;*
*Scenes of woe and scenes of pleasure,*
*Now a five years sad adieu."*

*In conclusion, I think I'm safe in saying that my homesick melancholy is "evanishing amid the storm" and bustle and furore my bodily size here occasions.*

*I am, your fond brother,*
*Angus MacAskill*

It is superfluous to add that this letter, though brief, was a source of consolation and congratulations.

Our hero wrote often to his friends, and dwelt long on themes which he judged interesting to them.

As this knowledge is obtainable from standard books

on travel, etc., it is not necessary to reproduce it here.

Ere long, the New Yorker procured him an unco' comrade. This was Tom Thumb, miniature phenomena, yes, the smallest full-grown man that ever lived. Tom Thumb was a fair dancer, and MacAskill would hold out his right arm and with the other he'd hoist Tom Thumb to the palm of his right hand. Here Tom Thumb would dance as merrily "as you please." Thereupon MacAskill would sometimes throw him into his pocket.

Tom Thumb was quite a joker. He'd put up his hand in boxing attitude sometimes, and challenge MacAskill to fight. This used to amuse MacAskill very much.

The chief towns of the provinces were visited in due time. The New Yorker often remarked: "The day I met MacAskill has proved to be a red-letter day in my life. My fortune is made, and moreover, he is such good company."

As railroads were not so plentiful then, they travelled much in coaches, but the roads being smooth their journeys were attended with comfort.

## Chapter XX

# MacAskill Travels Much

OUR HERO spent a short time in Cuba. It was then the depth of winter but the weather was still comfortably warm.

He was not very favourably impressed with Cuba. But as he said himself, if he had seen more of Cuban scenery, probably he might find something to admire.

He was not accustomed to travel much about the places at which he and his employer called, at least until the rush to see him was over. Were he to perambulate around, only a few would pay a dollar to see him thereafter as one good look at him would satiate curiosity to a bearable extent.

In the course of his travel, he met a man who was as tall as he himself, but almost as slender as a child. This man could walk in a dead calm, but the least wind would jeopardize his equilibrium. MacAskill averred that he was quite a sight. In fact, a gale might hoist that man "to the very clouds themselves."

He saw a darkey woman who was nearly as big as himself. Yes, she was almost his peer in height, stoutness and weight. As to her strength, there is nothing recorded thereabout.

We can easily conjecture that our hero saw many strange sights. Just fancy how delightful to spend a day in his company. Of course, be it said, that conversing over his reminiscences was no hobby of his. But, if courteously requested, he would willingly tell many stories of what he saw.

It may be remarked here that on his foreign tour he posed as a prodigy of size, not as a prodigy of strength. This was discreet, for had he chosen the latter, it might end very sadly. Hence, it was that he tried his strength but seldom during this undertaking.

He enjoyed his travels very much. He was not bashful and, under the gaze of thousands of spectators who came expressly to see him, he would stand up and walk around without evincing an iota of excitement.

No one ever went to see our hero to return disappointed, except in another sense of the word. They were usually agreeably disappointed. Yes, disappointed the right way, for them he was a greater show than they usually expected. This reminds one of a western man who got sick and came east soon recovered in our health-giving climate, and went back, as the papers chronicle, happily disappointed.

It does not belong to this book to give our hero's "tales

of travel" in full. But what has been stated will serve as a fitting sequel to the rest, which was not for the most part less interesting.

Many St. Ann's ladies and gentlemen can recall with pleasure, mellowed with a little sadness, the happy days they used to repair to our hero's home to listen to his marvellous stories.

## Chapter XXI

# He Verifies Reports About His Strength

THE PEOPLE of the United States, generally speaking, love their country and their countrymen to a remarkable degree. This is not unreasonable, for their country is a great one, and they have and have had their great men. But some Americans go so far as to ignore the idea that there are countries and men in other longitudes and latitudes as great as theirs.

The above remark is intended to warn the reader to be cautious in weighing the patriotic effusions of our friends "over the border." Let the Canadian study neutral statistics, and then decide for himself about the comparative greatness of the United States.

However, during our hero's sojourn in the United States, a friend of his and some Americans had a lively war of words about our hero's strength. Our hero's friend was one of those sturdy Cape Bretonians who say their say where they please, regardless of danger. Like Galcagus he possessed some of that stuff of which heroes are made. With his back to a brick edifice, gracefully posed, manly sounding the praises of MacAskill, he would remind one of James V of Scotland, as depicted by Scott, exclaiming:

"Come one, come all, this rock shall fly
From its firm base as soon as I."

At length the crowd dispersed, the greater number of them going into a wholesale liquor store near by. This friend of MacAskill's walked down the street. Turning a corner, whom did he meet but Angus MacAskill. It was a pleasant meeting. MacAskill was betimes told of the doubters. "Never mind," he said, "let us go to the store, and I may have a chance of impressing upon them the truth of the adage 'seeing is believing.'"

They arrived in the store. The crowd was still there. On seeing MacAskill, some of them fearing violence visibly trembled.

Our hero called for a drink for "all hands." While the rest were leisurely enjoying theirs he stepped over to a puncheon of Scotch Whiskey, containing one hundred and forty gallons. He lifted it on end. Then he struck the head a rap with his knuckles. The bung flew out and made skyward. Whereupon, he raised the puncheon, as if it were a jar, and drank to the health of the bystanders. Whether the drink was a large one or not is not known; it has not been recorded, but at least it was taken on the wholesale principle. However, having quaffed his, he paid for "all hands" and walked out.

The Americans of this episode were more than convinced, and declared that he ought to run for Congress, while the satisfaction of MacAskill's friend can only be fancied by those who had been repeatedly tantalized in a foreign land.

This achievement soon spread like a prairie fire never to die, and is listened to today in Australia and other parts by thousands of British descended people with a zest equal to our own.

## Chapter XXII

# He Visits Queen Victoria

IN THIS WORLD OF OURS, few exactly agree as to what character constitutes the ideal ruler. Perfect women and men are scarce. Hence the most loyal, not without reason, sometimes criticize their chief ruler rather unfavorably.

Again, and probably for the best, people differ in the nature and in the extent of deferential feelings towards their ruler. For instance, members of the British Empire are, as a rule, essentially loyal to the Queen, but few from the same motives. Some are loyal through personal affection, some through a love of the Queen's royalty, some through fear, some through appreciation of the Queen's policy, and others are loyal because they judge that, to an important extent, loyalty to the Queen is loyalty to themselves and to their interests. The last motive is decidedly the best. All men are born equal. Every woman and every man have a perfect right to be loyal to themselves. This granted, it goes without saying or demonstration that, if loyalty to a chief ruler is subversive to one's own interests, it is his or her duty, if opposed by the Throne, to seek and obtain redress or to hie to a less oppressive banner.

The idea of regarding chief rulers with great awe, sense of danger, etc., is erroneous. Should it come to the crisis that innocent men would be lawfully supposed to quake in presence of their ruler, surely any lady or gentleman could discern that there "was some rottenness in Denmark." Yes, readers, and remember that sovereigns are servants of the people, and are only to be honoured for the trust reposed in them and for their beneficial or praiseworthy services or achievements.

Loyalty should ever be governed by reason. The great

49

people of the world afford ample examples. Artemus Ward, for instance says, "bully for the national sentiment," but we cannot shout worth a cent on empty stomachs. The East Indian members of the British Empire could say likewise a year ago, when they were perishing in thousands while millions of dollars were being spent in other parts of the empire in the name of loyalty.

Speaking of extreme loyalty reminds one of a certain servant. His master did an extensive business and kept a ledger whose statements were sometimes doubted. When a customer was settling his account, should a dispute arise, the servant was at once telephoned by his master, when the following dialogue would take place: "Hello!" "Yes, sir." "Will you swear to this?" "Yes, sir; yes, what is it?"

But reverting to the character best fitted to rule, we are many. As already said, few of us exactly agree on that point. But our noble Queen Victoria is truly great and possessed of the dignity that becomes her charge as well as that humility that endears her to us, so that the attitude of one and all towards her is like that of his flock to Goldsmith's village preacher.

Queen Victoria is a great personage. That she is a queen adds not much to her splendour. For, in the words of Shakespeare, the king of dramatic poetry:

"My crown is in my heart, not on my head;
Not decked with diamonds and Indian stones,
Nor to be seen. My Crown is called Content—
A crown it is that seldom kings enjoy."

But enough. However, be it announced that Her Majesty Queen Victoria invited Angus MacAskill to Windsor Castle. He soon called upon her. She gave him a cordial reception. She chatted pleasantly with him for a few hours.

She was highly interested in his great size, and complimented him very warmly. She presented him with two rings of gold.

MacAskill regretted that there were no means of showing his power of lifting, but he thought of a plan to leave a token of his strength on the sly. He walked back and forth before the Queen, secretly pressing the carpet with his heels. When he left, the carpet, though thick and strong, was cut here and there in the bread cutter fashion, by the heels of the giant.

The Queen said afterwards that he was the tallest, the stoutest and the strongest man that ever entered the palace.

MacAskill was well pleased with his visit. Yet he was not intoxicated by the honour, but preserved his wonted composure. 'Tis true, her kindness increased and enlived his love for her, yet there were others he loved best, loyal as he was. Chief among those were his parents and his brothers and sisters.

Still our hero was a model of loyalty, but, in ordinary matters, with him "the man was the gold and all that."

## Chapter XXIII

# He Goes to Edinburgh

OUR HERO'S VISIT to Edinburgh interested him very much. Edinburgh is brimful of interest, not mere curiosity, but genuine sensible interest. There one may see plenteous tokens of the varied trains of thought, study and activity which have prevailed in the ages that have been. If there be "a whim-inspired fool" who supposes that the Scotch have been uncivilized in any age, let him go to Edinburgh. There, the mist which constitutes such a supposition will be dissolved forever by the light of revelations which convince.

Before proceeding further, it may not be amiss to refer to one of Scotland's giants and heroes, Sir William Wallace. This was an "extraordinary man." Historically, it is not very long since Wallace lived and died, yet a great many lies have been manufactured about him. Jane Porter wrote a novel called *Scottish Chiefs*, in which Wallace figured, and strange to say some suppose that novel to be a true story. Jane Porter is not to be blamed for this, I presume, but it is a recognized fact and a happy one that the truth about Wallace is more interesting than the brightest inventions of fiction, and it is to be regretted that such an able writer as Jane Porter did not write a true life of Wallace in addition to her famous novel, *Scottish Chiefs*.

Sir William Wallace flourished in the thirteenth century. He was uncommonly stout, tall, heavy, muscular, strong, brave and full of life. His patriotism will be remembered with undecreasing appreciation while time exists.

Among the first exploits of Wallace was the killing of a few English armed warriors. The Scotchman's only weapon was a fishing rod.

It may be remembered that in these days the English kings strongly desired to rule Scotland. Wallace from the cradle up was strongly opposed to English rule. Some of the English soldiers and sentinels sent to Scotland were too haughty and insolent, hence the episode recorded above.

Wallace marshalled an army in due time, and was very successful against the English. In 1297, at the famous battle of Sterling Bridge, he utterly routed the English Governor of Scotland. "Soon not an English soldier remained north of the Tweed, and Wallace was elected Governor of Scotland."

"For eight years, in spite of the coldness and jealousy of the nobility, he ably maintained Scotland's cause. At last he was betrayed by a false friend, and hanged in London in 1305 A.D." — See *Brief History of England*.

The King of France once requested Wallace to cross

over with a few officers to help him against a certain country. Wallace consented. He and a nephew of his and a few more soon went aboard a ship and sailed. Soon the red sails of the fleet of a well known sea pirate hove in sight. He was known as the Red Rover. The captain was shocked. Wallace said, "Fear nothing." Wallace asked the captain if he knew the Red Rover.

The captain said, "Yes." Wallace said, "Describe his appearance." The captain said, "He's a great man about your size, and as a distinction wears a red woolen coat over his mail. Moreover he is usually the first man to jump aboard the prey." "That will do," said Wallace, "you and your men go and hide." Then he ordered his own men to go down below except his beloved nephew. Wallace and his nephew paced the deck, waiting for the Red Rover.

They had not to wait long. In jumped the Red Rover, Wallace grabbed him, and, ladies and gentlemen, that was a tussle. Soon the Red Rover's heels described a semi-circle in the air; down comes the Red Rover on his face on deck. Wallace seized him by the back of the neck and knocked the deck with his mouth. "Who are you?" gasped the pirate. "I am Wallace of Scotland," was the reply. "And the strongest man I ever met," said the Red Rover. "But I'm your man now and henceforth," added the Red Rover. He was as good as his word. He bravely fought under Wallace in France, and afterwards in Scotland, and was one of King Robert Bruce's right hand men at the battle of Bannockburn.

The sword of Wallace ranks among the wonders of the world. Nine inches were accidently broken off the top. The two parts may be seen in Edinburgh. The sword was seven feet in length and wide proportionately. Hugh Gillis, warden of Upper Margaree, interviewed two reputable men who actually saw and handled the sword of Wallace. Both men's descriptions exactly agreed. Both these men declared that it weighed forty pounds. After the death of Wallace, his sword was treasured in Dumfries for hundreds of years.

In the reign of good King George the Fourth on the occasion of his visit to Edinburgh, the memorable sword of Wallace, that the King might see it, was taken there, and there it is today.

MacAskill went to see the sword of Wallace. He said he could possibly wield it on the battlefield, but that it was rather big and heavy.

Now, gentle reader, think of the man who could wield it as easily as you could a bayonet. But it is gratifying to know MacAskill was the only man who could swing and brandish it in the martial style except the great Sir William Wallace himself.

But a few words about Dumfries City. Here lies buried one of Scotland's intellectual giants, Robert Burns. He was a great poet. Notwithstanding his naturally strong and rebellious passions, he lived a good life, a life of current sobriety, a life of superfluous honesty, and died happily, attended by his wife, Bonnie Jean, and by his lovely friend, Jessie Lewyars.

Edinburgh, Dumfries, etc., were visited by MacAskill. The most of them pleased him very much but Edinburgh the most of all.

## Chapter XXIV

# He Shoulders a Monster Weight

THE ANCHOR EXPLOIT of Angus MacAskill was truly wonderful. The author has read and heard more than one account thereof. Of these he will narrate merely two, which, though differing in details, agree essentially. However, the second version given is more authentic, and, in fact, there is no reason to doubt its truthfulness.

The first version says that on a New York pier, there was an anchor weighing twenty-two hundred pounds. MacAskill came here one day and met some French sailors. After chatting for some time, the conversation drifted to the big anchor. The Frenchmen had heard before of our hero's strength, and wanted to see it tested. They said that they knew a giant in France who could shoulder it, and spoke in words as to say that a man from St. Ann's, Cape Breton, could not move it.

Our hero caught the anchor, shouldered it and poised it on his shoulder with ease, to the surprise of the Frenchmen. They had not expected that. Be it said also that their French giant story was but a fib to trick MacAskill into trying his strength. The author does not intend to try to justify them, but their motives, if dishonest might have been more patriotic than criminal. But sad to say, when MacAskill threw the anchor off, one of the flukes caught him in the shoulder region, and shattered his massive constitution forever.

The second version has no French connected therewith. But this is not what makes it preferable but that it is very probably the truth entirely.

To begin, the famous anchor weighed two thousand seven hundred. It was lying on a New York pier. Why it was disused at the time is not now known.

Our hero went to the pier one evening, and for pastime grabbed the anchor, and with startling ease raised it. He did not tremble; his face did not redden. He walked back and forth with the ponderous anchor on his shoulder.

Little did he know "that soon, too soon," his blooming constitution was going to be blighted forever. But it is a good thing that "coming events" do not "cast their shadows before." Were people to know their future, the knowledge might be, if not always sad, yet a little more embarrassing.

Our hero as already said paced the pier, and at length tossed the anchor as if it were an ordinary cable, but one of the flukes hooked his shoulder, and wrecked his stalwart frame.

The bystanders all were in tears. He was in great pain for a while. In course of time he improved to some extent.

In another chapter it will be seen whether or not this wrecking accident was so significant to his strength as a miniature accident would be to an ordinary man.

## Chapter XXV

# Other Giants

IT IS PROPER to announce that we have had, and have in Cape Breton, and in the peninsula of Nova Scotia, scores of giants, though none of them could be compared with MacAskill. Some of them have been or are giants of size and strength, others giants in strength alone. We find them descended from various nationalities, Irish, French, Scotch and English.

Neil MacDonald, of Kirkwood, Lake Ainslie, was one of these. In Margaree Harbour he turned a cannon weighing perhaps fifteen hundred, end over end, somersault so to speak. His son, Dr. H. N. MacDonald, is one of the ablest athletes in the world to-day. He is as strong as nine or ten men, and full of life and beautiful physique.

Charles MacLear (Alex's son) formerly of Scotsville, was an able-bodied man. He went to Klondyke, but was never heard from, and possibly perished.

John H. Gillis, of Scotsville, is a modern giant of strength. He lifts very heavy weights with surprising ease.

The late John Gillis (Peter's son), S. W. Margaree, is six feet six inches in height, and weighs proportionately. He performed exploits of which no Cape Bretonian of Nova Scotia need be ashamed. A large spruce log he can handle like a long shingle block.

The MacFarlanes, Gillis', MacDougalls, MacDonells and Camerons of Upper and S. W. Margaree have and have had giants in their ranks, that would grace a royal guard. These fought too (I do not mean among themselves), and, figuratively speaking, sheathed their swords, but for want of argument.

Broad Cove, Mabou, Port Hood, Judique, Port Hastings and Hawkesbury, Whycocomagh, etc., have had and have giants.

Margaree Forks, Emerald, N. E. Margaree, M. Harbour, Friar's Head and Cheticamp have their celebrities. The late Mr. Brussard (Jno. Brussard's father), of Margaree Forks, has had but few equals. One day he hauled a plough by the side of an ox for six hours. The McKinnons of East and West Ainslie, will be ever famous. Again at Upper East Ainslie, there is an unassuming man, Allan MacDougall by name, who if attacked would prove to be a terror.

Again, L.E. MacLean, Black River; Charles L. MacDonald, of Kirkwood, Lake Ainslie; Allan MacQuarrie, of Loch Ban; Michael Kennedy, of Loch Ban; Simon MacDonell, S. W. Margaree; Thomas Dunbar, North Ainslie; Ronald MacLellan, Egypt; Donald R. MacLean, Broad Cove Mines, S. W. Margaree; Duncan A. MacLellan, S. W. Margaree; John J. MacDonald, S. W. Margaree; John J. Gillis, S. W. Margaree, are all men who grace our island chivalry. Victoria County is not wanting in fine bodied men. MacCharles and others have wrestled laurels from competitors of high order.

Cape Breton County and Richmond raise stalwart boys too.

Throughout the peninsula (Nova Scotia proper) an exceptionally strong man is not a strange sight.

But a few Cape Bretonians are still mentioned. One of these is the late Allan MacDonell, of Mount Pleasant, Upper Margaree, whom the late Neil MacDonald of Kirkwood, Lake Ainslie, reputed to be the strongest man to lift a weight he ever met, and Archibald Gillis and Angus MacNeil, of Broad Cove, two who will never know to perfection what they can lift and what they can't.

This chapter, far from lessening Angus MacAskill in appreciation, will, on the contrary, serve to convince the reader of the truth of what is related of our hero. And, moreover, the modern "instances" are interesting in themselves.

The author, however, apologizes for using some names without asking for consent, but he opines that his friends alluded to are too lenient to criticise this, and much too lenient to criticise "the style in which it's done." —Farewell.

**Chapter XXVI**

# A Trip From Upper Margaree to Margaree Harbour

THE AUTHOR OF THIS BOOK on being informed that Angus MacDougall, of Margaree Harbour, had worked for Angus MacAskill, set off to interview Mr. MacDougall on a fine October morning.

The sun was just peeping over the Egyptian mountains to smile on Kiltarlity, as I directed my steps northward. The landscape views that seemed to present themselves voluntarily to my gaze in close succession were near to perfection, at least if my judgment of perfection be taken as a standard.

The road was soon alive and abustle with girls and boys, horses and buggies, bicycles, etc. Soon a gentleman from North Ainslie, John C. Campbell, sailed along in a horse car. He told me to jump in, and I did. I soon learned that he was en route for Mr. Murphy's with apples.

After half an hour's travel over the smooth road we arrived at Mr. Murphy's. Mr. Murphy was away from home, but none the less I enjoyed my call very highly, and so did Mr. Campbell.

Our hostess (Mr. Murphy's housewife), a beautiful magnetic young lady of excellent disposition, rallied us with pleasing talk and a delicious repast. This over, Mr. Campbell treated us with apples, announcing to our hostess (Miss Ross), at the same time that he was marketing apples, moreover. The bargain was soon transacted. Mr. Campbell made quite a wholesale that morning; in fact, he sold the entire load, eight barrels, right there and then. While the hired man was removing them to the storehouse, I bade my hostess and Mr. Campbell a fond good morning.

Being in very good humour, I walked briskly, and soon sighted Margaree Forks. Margaree Forks has been so often described that further descriptions are unnecessary. In due time I tipped the door-bell of Hugh Gillis' residence. I was well entertained, stayed overnight, and took the road the next morning at "break of day."

About seven o'clock I was at my destination. Mr. and Mrs. Angus MacDougall reside about a mile south of Margaree Harbour town. They are a kindly couple, and soon regaled me with news, anecdotes and a profuse table.

The brandy bottle was produced, but as I declined its intimacy (being a teetotaler), it was set aside. Talk of hospitality, but they are lovely. In due time I related the object of my visit. Mr. MacDougall took the matter seriously, and was silent and abstracted for an hour or more, and then told his story of MacAskill. In some minor points it differed with my data, but they were essentially identical.

Next morning, "happy be the day," I left for Upper Margaree. My friend MacDougall drove me to Margaree Forks. An hour and a half's walk brought me to S. W. Margaree. I could not resist the inclination to call where I had called in my northward transit, and, in fact, I did not try.

"I'll ne'er blame my partial fancy,
Nothing could resist my Nancy;
But to see her was to love her,
Love but her and love forever."

Shortly after noon, however, I was on the road again. Betimes, I was back in Upper Margaree. Though I don't owe my birth to this settlement (being born at Strathlorne), however, as I passed many years here, I may be permitted to say that it is a beauty.

Mountains, glens, rocks and valleys, intersected with streams of becoming size; clearances, houses, barns, wood factories and forests—all these are here, as it were in semi-careless profusion. The homes of Upper Margaree, so plenteous in wealth and cheer, are generally ornaments that would set off any country to advantage.

Gentle reader, if such scenery be not truly lovely—loveliness upon our earth is surely rare.

## Chapter XXVII

# MacAskill After His Return and His Death

ANGUS MACASKILL was well paid by the New Yorker with whom he travelled. Hence, when he came home to St. Ann's he possessed a snug fortune.

He donated respectable sums to many of his relatives and friends. Of course, none of these were poor before, but the gifts of our hero were none the less acceptable, and some of them were appreciated as intensely as Napoleon Bonaparte's gift to Campbell's English sailor.

He filled the role of a second Marc Lescarbot by building two good grist-mills a suitable distance apart. This undertaking proved very profitable.

He was an accomplished miller, and at times ran one of his mills himself. The other was in charge of Angus MacDougall, at present of Margaree Harbour.

It was interesting to see Angus MacAskill, while picking the millstones, hold the pick between his thumb and two fingers. It need not be said that he would turn over the stones with as much ease as a Scotch-descended Cape Breton bonnie lassie would turn over a sugar loaf.

As for wheat bags, oat bags, etc., some containing four bushels, they were mere playthings in his hands.

Were the mill brook to run dry, and flour or meal to become scarce, provided that there was grain on hand, he could avert a temporary embarrassment by driving the mill himself. He could easily turn the pit-wheel round for hours, if necessary, or tear off the cogs.

He built an elegant store and stocked it well, and kept it so. He was a reputable business man, honest, prompt and agreeable. He sold his goods at a low figure, and thus, though not intentionally, he, like Sir Richard Arkright, relieved the sails of other merchants of some wind. He never admired the credit system, and in business he never encouraged its adoption, yet, he never refused to help a person in need, be he an acquaintance or a stranger.

His ledger, etc., are still extant, and evince a practical knowledge of commercial bookkeeping. Yet, today, from the fact that L.s.d., are there instead of $ and ¢, they may appear a little quaint.

At St. Ann's you may see the great Angus MacAskill's store. There it is, a momento of a glorious past, but unoccupied. How many a heart overflowing with gratitude departed from that store. Our hero and many of his customers have gone to their reward; but are they forgotten? No. And while a vestige of that edifice graces the landscape, it will recall to the minds of one and all, MacAskill's life, MacAskill's charity and MacAskill's philanthropy, and thereby associate our hearts with trains of thought fully as beneficial and ennobling as Goldsmith's Deserted Village.

By the way, the doors of the store bear future evidence to our hero's overhead requirements. They are nine feet in height, and his favorite stool is there. What do you suppose it is? It is a 180-gallon molasses puncheon.

It has been already said that the anchor seriously hurt our hero. In fact, his frame was permanently shattered. Possibly his backbone was injured, and probably some of his ribs displaced. He could never afterwards stand straightly erect, and raising from a chair to a standing position was always a matter of difficulty, and at times of torture.

But still his strength was prodigious, a fact which he occasionally manifested. Now and again some people would fancy that his strength was failing down to the ordinary. But ho! my friends, some new exploits would more than dispel these visions.

The anchor exploit already portrayed and his subsequent ones excited more than usual interest because he had previously a severe fever in Spain. This malady had impaired his constitution forever, and lessened his strength over twenty percent. Therefore, the anchor exploit may be pronounced doubly wonderful, and his later exploits trebly wonderful.

But, regarding his exploits, they were all astonishing. Hence, all who have heard of them and of their hero, MacAskill, take pleasure in treasuring mementos or remembrances of his strength and size. At Donald McKay's, blacksmith, Scotsville, one of the family, Thomas McKay, showed me an inner boot sole of MacAskill's. This sole I measured, and its size was not contradictory to my earlier researches. About Genoa, the poet Rogers began:

"Reader, if thou should'st come to Modena," but I say, Reader, if thou should'st ever come to Scotsville, stop at Donald MacKay's and ask to see the sole mentioned, and you will, and, moreover, receive what Robert Burns desired to receive in Heaven—"a Highland welcome."

However, in August, 1863, Angus MacAskill was seized with that dire ailment, brain fever. The disease set in without any apparent cause.

It is gratifying to know that medical science and art were timely exerted to their utmost to save his life, or, at least, to prolong it, but in vain. Shortly before death, all delirium left him. Indeed, for a few hours he enjoyed sweet tranquility, and conversed with those around him. Yet he was woefully weak, and he thought that the end was near.

On the 8th of August, after a week's illness, he expired as a child falls into a peaceful sleep. The pastor of the place was present. Though confident that his soul was in "the better land," yet all around were in tears.

The news of our hero's death spread like wild-fire. Sympathetic messages were received by his sisters and brothers, and were promptly acknowledged.

Notwithstanding the furore caused by our hero's size

and strength in the days gone by, so great was sorrow and excitement occasioned and aroused by his death that his most intense native admirers were surprised.

Newspaper after newspaper told the tale of the death of the Cape Breton giant. Encomiums were showered on his memory.

His sisters and brothers bore their affection with great patience. The sting of death was sore indeed; but they were sensible enough to see that they had many consolations. Our hero had died in their midst "with comforts at his side." His life and death were edifying. These consolations soon relieved and in due time completely healed that horrid wound—the recollection of a friend's death.

## Chapter XXVIII

# The Coffin

AFTER OUR HERO'S DEATH, among the first things considered was a coffin. In those times imported coffins were not yet dreamed of. Two reputable carpenters undertook to make the coffin, and they had it completed in six hours.

The coffin was made of native pine boards, as coffins usually were in the days when pine was plentiful. The cover was one-fourth glass. In size the coffin was the sight of a life time. Yet, so well proportioned was it that it looked uncouth by no means. Yes, it seemed to be smaller than what an actual measurement would attest.

It was costly lined with white cloth. Great pains were taken with every detail. Accomplished ladies and gentlemen thus vied with one another in showing their respect, admiration, and appreciation of this extraordinary man.

The exterior of the coffin was lovely. The bright mountings shone out in harmonious contrast with the sober dark ground which they embellished.

In due time the sad task of laying our hero's remains in their last earthly home was becomingly performed. The lid being replaced, the spectators in dozens paced orderly along once more to gaze "on the face that was dead." Bouquets and wreaths without number were brought along. An aged aristocratic man present who had spent years in Edinburgh said: "I have seen many a coffin; but if this is not the costliest coffin I have seen, it is the most beautiful and the best festooned. These bouquets would do honour to a prince. Never have I seen such genuine and sensible indications of sorrow as MacAskill's mourners have evinced."

The minister of the congregation arrived at the appointed hour. After prayer and scriptural reading he preached an appropriate sermon. His Christian and modest eulogy of our hero will long be remembered.

During the sermon many wept. But ere he had neared the end, the mists of sadness began to dissolve "like the dim fabric of a vision," and when the moment of the benediction arrived, there was not a sad heart in the crowd.

But reverting to the coffin, the reader has probably by this time formed an idea thereof in his or her mind. The beauty of it can be imaged by comparisons or "modern instances." But to imagine its size is very difficult.

It has been said that figures speak. This is a true saying. Yet the actual dimensions of our hero's coffin need not be given, another way of communicating an idea of its size being judged, more easily grasped, and more easily remembered moreover.

Hence, an emphatic illustration is chosen to convey the idea, not at all as a substitute, but as a better medium of this knowledge. Figures may be forgotten, but the following disclosure never.

When the woodwork of the coffin was finished i.e., when it was ready for the dressing, etc., it was found to be sufficient to bear or float three men across the Bay of St. Ann's.

How this has transpired is left to the readers as a matter of conjecture. However, it serves as an additional argument in support of the far-famed saying "truth is stranger than fiction."

## Chapter XXIX

# MacAskill's Grave

ON THE EASTERN SIDE of St. Ann's Bay, about a mile and a half from the sea, there is a bonnie cemetery. As you go down by the bay, facing north, it is on your right side. Less than a mile to the south of it, on your left hand side, is one of St. Ann's churches, a magnificent building, with a vane on the top of the spire, which tells the observer there the four fundamental points of a compass, and what's of little less importance "the way the wind blows."

The church referred to above, to aid the stranger in locating the cemetery without asking too many questions. Strangers who are extremely modest like to be spared the odium of asking questions on every side.

Close by the road the cemetery begins. It continues quite a distance up a brae or hillside, then curves over to the top of a hill, and you are on the level, and a few yards ahead you observe its western boundary.

In this cemetery the vegetable kingdom is profusely represented. There are elder bushes, cherry trees, raspberry bushes, low wild-rose bushes, and many other beauties of the kind. It reminds one of a passage that we read in Lucy Flemming—that quaint, though happy phrase, "its cheerful graves."

On the upper level of the cemetery, a mound of earth twelve feet in length artistically set off with gravel and a respectable gravestone mark the earthly resting place of our hero.

A few feet to the north-east of it are the graves of Mr. and Mrs. Abraham MacIntosh. Rev. Mr. MacIntosh was a pastor of St. Ann's and North Shore. He died on March 10, 1889. His wife's maiden name was Annie Ross. She was born in 1822, and died in 1884. There is a becoming paling yard around their graves. Lastly, there's a superb monument, which, if not necessary to perpetuate the memory of their virtues, designates to the tourist their cosy abode at the top of the hill of life which, like John Anderson and his wife, they well "had climbed together."

The breath of St. Ann's cemetery is as fragrant and sweet as that of a flower garden. As one walks along he is apt to imagine that a costly deodorant has been sprinkled about a few minutes ago.

But let us go back to our hero's grave and read the inscription so deftly carved on yonder stone. Here it is in toto:

Erected

to

the memory of

Angus MacAskill

The Nova Scotian Giant

Who died, August 8th, 1863

Aged 38 years.

A dutiful son, a kind brother. Just in all his dealings.
Universally respected by friends and acquaintances.
"Mark the perfect man and behold the upright,
The end of that man is peace."

Opposite the cemetery is a little sandy island ornamented by a lighthouse, elsewhere referred to. On the west side of the bay, opposite the cemetery, a moderately high and rather steep mountain begins at the water's edge. Here, half a mile or so of the mountain side is still wooded and uninhabited, and exhibits a relieving contrast with the great remainder domesticated by the hand of man.

## Chapter XXX

# Duncan MacAskill's Description of Our Hero

ONE OF OUR HERO'S BROTHERS, an excellent man, Duncan MacAskill by name, when interviewed has had the following to say about our hero's appearance, in addition to what you have read:

"My brother's hair was very black and curly. Otherwise he was light complexioned. His face was freckled."

Now, it was a little singular that his hair was very dark, while his arms, etc., were light complexioned. Yet we meet with such cases now and then. A peculiarity pertaining to a celebrated person glistens more conspicuously. If you meet an ordinary man at a house, or on a train, except in special cases, you don't scrutinize his appearance; but if you meet Sir Charles Tupper, the Earl of Minto, or President MacKinley, or Queen Victoria, all your observing facilities are quickly employed. You scan and mentally analyse every feature, and, if you see any peculiarity, it is never to be effaced from your memory. Hence, it is that we exclaim, "how strange," when told that Angus MacAskill's head was black, whereas his arms were light complexioned.

Can medical science account for all the causes of freckles? However, freckles seldom deduct very materially from a person's beauty. Nevertheless freckles are not desired; but freckle-faced people have this consolation, viz., only snow white skin becomes freckled. With those who work in the sun, the absence of freckles indicates a skin tinged a little like Klondike currency.

Again his brother adds:

"My brother's facial features were well-proportioned. His mouth was pretty. His lips were fairly thin and rosy. He had a good chin, red cheeks, a well shaped head. His neck was stout and not over long. He dressed 'stylishly' but was not painfully careful in dressing himself."

A glance at his picture will corroborate these above remarks. We may suppose that Angus MacAskill was handsome. He was a lovely giant. In this, he a real giant, differed from the giants that we are apt to picture for ourselves in our imagination.

'Twas pleasant to see this great big man so gentlemanly in appearance. Of course, his merit and good character were emphatically more important, but a winning appearance helped to set off the man to better advantage.

Finally, his brother said:

"When my brother put on the highland costume, which, by the way, was a present from Queen Victoria (not that he was my brother), but he looked like one of those heroes we read of in the ancient chronicles."

Giant Angus MacAskill's gravestone at Englishtown, erected by the Nova Scotia government about fifty years after his death. The original stone (from which Gillis copied the inscription on page 67) is on display at The Giant MacAskill Museum, at Englishtown.

# Other Writings

## by James D. Gillis

JAMES MARTELL OF THE NOVA SCOTIA Public Archives visited James D. Gillis at Melrose Hill and took some photographs of him.

Gillis was sitting in a rocking chair outside his small house, wearing three sweaters, heavy socks pulled over his trousers, gum rubbers on his feet—and playing the violin. He insisted that Martell photograph him not only from the front and sides, but also from behind.

"In case," Gillis explained, "some day a statue is raised to my honour. The back view would be a great help to the sculptor."

The Author, James D. Gillis, at his home on Mount Young

# A Little Sketch of My Life

I WAS BORN JULY 11, 1870. At this time my parents lived at Broad Cove Intervale near Strathlorne. Formerly they had homesteaded at Grand Mira. My father was a house painter and a blacksmith. He was also a noted violinist and piper and a wit. My mother, Christina MacAulay, was descended from the MacAulays of N. Uist and a distant relative (it seems) of Lord MacAulay.

When I was seven months old, my father died. Then I was removed to Upper Margaree, where I climbed the years of probation.

When I was born I had my first teeth and my mother often remarked that people then said that this was a sign that I'd be a poet.

At the age of 5 I read the 4th book. This book corresponded to the 3rd Royal of a later period. In short at that time I could read any English book and my reason would divine the meaning of hard words. Inspector Jno. Y. Gunn said I had a good memory. But my reasoning powers were far superior. A noted scholar from Scotland (from Kircudbright) said I resembled Sir Walter Scott, my forehead etc.

I never cared for taking things on authority. I abominated ambiguous problems. If left to myself I could solve any problem as well or better than I can today tho I have solved and straightened out some useless and puzzling ones. But much of the education of many years was coming and going. On Grammar and Composition in early years I saw the idea of function and it consoles me now to see others at long last come to this although they never ascribe any credit to me. But I see a few writers on Gram. theory try to twine our hard fought for English with college made Italian usefully designated Latin. It is absolutely impossible that any nation of that age or any other would move among such a machine of a Language as that. When I think of all our boys of all generations did for our language, I blush to think of grammars with Non. Case, Dative Case, Ablative Case, Accusative Case, supines, etc.

But enough. At eighteen I opened school at Big Cove Banks. I taught the largest at MacFarlane's Bridge, Piper's Glen, N. Ainslie, Judique Intervale, Miller Sec. (Melrose Hill) and Sask.

Among pupils are Rev. M. McCormack, East Bay; Rev. Flavian Sampson, L'Ardoise, N. S.; Rev. Chas. Alison McKenzie; Rev. Arch. D. McKinnon, Lake Ainslie; Prof. Murdoch C. McLean, Sc. Dept. Ottawa; Rodk. McLean Kenlock, merchant.

1. I may issue a biography—a fiction before Xmas.

2. I am not married. I don't approve of love at first sight. I think divorce as justifiable as swearing, etc., i.e., if there be grave reasons.

3. I favor sports and "physical exercises" as prescribed for schools; but I don't approve of the diplomacy shown by inspectors in giving prizes. The judge should be a Sergeant of the Militia or Permanent Force. We are too well acquainted with the prize to

1 Religious Sister Cath.
1 Teacher in a town. A Prot.
1 Cath.    pet    Balance carried forward
1 Prot.    pet      —where?
1 Another politics pet.

But all harmless sports I approve of. I can fish, swim, walk on stilts. I can't cycle. I seldom play cards.

3. I farmed some and worked in the lumberwoods in an Insane Hosp. And was watchman at Simpsons, Regina.

4. I issued the *C. B. Giant* 1898. It was printed by Jno. Lovell & Son, Montreal. I sold the rights to Messrs. T. C. Allen & Co. Halifax in 1907.

I issued *Modern English or (Can. Gram.)* in 1904, and not long after sold the rights to Messrs. T. C. Allen.—Printer A. C. Bertram Prop. N. S. Herald.

I issued the *Great Election* in 1915, sold many copies here and there by mail and later the rest, something less than 1000 copies to Messrs. T. C. Allen.

I made the *C. B. Author's Map of the World, — the 4 pole map* — in 1905. A. G. DesBrisay was the draftsman and he made all the blue prints I desired. It was entered in Stationer's Hall, London, England.

5. I liked the N. School at Truro very much. Mr. Benoit, Dr. Hall and Dr. Soloan used me very well. At this school with those professors my perspicacity and native ability reasoning powers etc. served me just as well as when I was under 12. They could answer and could answer any question, would joke, never stabbed in the back by false reports to Halifax, etc., etc. They were men and took responsibilities, — never hinted that the Supt. constrained them to do this or that. Yes, they were none of those sneaking cowards who regret they have to command this or that and then refer to the absent man of authority. It was no Summer School of Science where a group of quack scientists and an inspector organize a school Annual Meeting to ridicule the poor of their native land to whom those cravens look for protection in times of danger and then try to smatter out a few Gaelic words, when the Saxon talk has rebounded in sad echo from the Saxon funnel of the Saxony submarine.

In Saskatchewan and Alberta I taught school for 6 years; from the view-point of scholars, parents and trustees with great success, and according to the views of school inspectors from Ontario, with poor success. I took charge of schools that were in a forlorn state and left everything O. K. and the children much improved. In one inspector's learned report I was held responsible for things that occurred years before I left N. S. Others were contented to gasp that I was untidy, poorly clad, etc., etc., anything at all to put me down. Those insp. are commanded to live in their inspectorate but they live in Regina. We forget down here that the Prairie Provinces belong to Ontario and Germany. So look out for those little great men.

Sir Wilfred Laurier set Alberta and Saskatchewan agoing in 1905. Now those owners have sunk Saskatchewan down in a debt that never will be paid. So much for a govt. that approves of such school officials. In Alberta my school was visited by an inspector, an Acadian from Inv. Co. N. S. He said, "I am J. T. Ross of the Educ. Dpt., Edmonton." This Insp. favored a band of Trustees that were not in the habit of paying teachers; but one of them later had to decamp. I might say this was certainly not Mr. Ross but Mr. White. He too away from his inspectorate lived in Edmonton. It would pay to travel from N. S. to Regina and Edmon. to see the cleanliness and pride of those inspectors. His Majesty King Geo. when inspecting troops would seem nothing compared with those and as for their powers as teachers they laid claims to probity etc. that could do justice to a Chief of the Metis or Crees. The high opinion those inspectors have of themselves should be ranked among the seven wonders of the world. They too show great diplomacy re Strathcona prizes, viz.

1 Nun
1 Red Cross Nurse
1 Prot.
1 Cath.
1 Menonite
1 Dookabor

The same number of each sex. Prizes are divided over the Provinces and inspectorates according to diplomacy.

Inspectors can do anything. If a school board refuses to accept a married teacher from Ontario the Inspector cancels the trustees and appoints himself or somebody else trustee at $50 or more a year. He can make and unmake teachers. He can judge clothes. If a suit from the Tiptop Tailors doesn't fit a teacher, he reports this to "papa," the Deputy Min. of Educ. There is a Compulsory Attendance law but if a child runs 40 miles on a school day after a binder the teacher is blamed for this, but the law sets inspectors above law.

Reverting to myself—early in life my education was interrupted by the pulling down of the old school-house and the building of a new. After the age of 13, the number of days I went to school were few.

I can read music, staff and tonic sol fa, and can play the violin and bag-pipe.

Among men who influenced me I mention Jas. A. McFarlane, Donald MacLennan, barrister, Angus R. McLennan, teacher, now abroad, William T. Allen, Halifax, William

Alexander J. MacLean, Strathlorne, Jno. A. MacDougall, B. Cove Banks, Donald A. MacDonnell, Kiltarlity, Upper Margaree, Drs. Hall and Soloan, Truro, Cpt. Borden, Halifax, Major Doull, Halifax, Co. Cpt. W. McKenzie, Iron Mines, Dr. A. H. McKay, Halifax, Andro Turto Alvena, Sask., and Mr. S. Kaiff, Simpson Bldg., Regina.

I compose best in solitude. I don't like to write on any subject by request. But if thoughts and conclusions occupy me for years, I write these with ease. Original terms, idioms etc. crowd on one another and for fear of misunderstanding I sometimes change the expression to the vogue of the hour. Yet, I believe that my natural expression has more punch than a modified. I avoid exaggeration and leave out lots that might be written. For a prosaic example if Mr. Stone weighed 200 lb., I write he weighed at least 150 etc., etc. When A or B investigates the result produces confidence. This manner of probability (in truth) enhances fiction itself. A novel may contain more interesting episodes, than are known of an ordinary life; but none of the episodes should be unnatural or impossible. As far as we know, Nelson, James IV, Scipio, Hannibal, Napoleon I, etc. were simply good, meek boys and men who did their part. Fictitious characters to be interesting or valuable should lead lives, practical and practicable.

In politics I favor the Liberal party. I don't approve of Confederation. It was made for Quebec and Ontario. It ruined the Maritime Prov. and B. C. If N. S. had a chance, today she would vie with Maine or Mass., U. S. But it's Ontario and other parts of the "Empire" first. Yes but we have the C. P. R. and the C. N. R. They are of no more help to N. S. than they are to Cuba or Nfld. I am opposed to life jobs. No Govt. office of any kind should be held by one person or family for more than 10 years, Judgeship, Inspectorship, P. O. Office, Custom Office etc., Councillor, M. P. P., M. P. and at that those should be elected at the polls.

# *from* **The Great Election**
## *from the* **Introduction**

THERE IS ONE THING that we ought to foster more here, and that is equality. As long as a man is civil and proper be he rich or poor, foreigner, anything, we owe him cheerful respect, courtesy, and his rights. When we come in contact with people it is not wise to grade or judge them.

In this matter it is not necessary to insult persons of proved genius, tact or learning. As we may commend, reward or compliment such without offence to others. Yes, for equality does not imply that we are identically equal, but it does imply that we recognize one another's rights and live moral lives in subordination to nobody....

The public schools in their interior life have upheld equality. Yet the Boards of Trustees are not always perfectly impartial. This tends to intrude a shallow mercenary feeling into the young which precipitates them into minor affairs and diverts them from the deep exploration both of their own powers and the fathomless recesses of our noble land.

The schools recognized women as fit to teach. Later the colleges recognized them, tho they are a little slow in appointing them professors.

It is strange that often those who are very polite before ladies, and bother others in their excited ado before ladies, it is strange that these and their kind have never done anything for equality. Their seeming ardor is but an impulse which depends entirely on the presence of the ladies and their attitude.

The cause of the suffragettes is good. We want all men and women everywhere. We want women as Members of Parliament, Attendants, Doctors, Lawyers, Lecturers, etc. We want worthy poor men in every position man can fill. This is the spirit of our age. Let the future see that ours was the reform.

# Second Poet

I loved to sing since time was young
The old, the new and all in song
The Scotch songs I loved them all
Fair Birdie loved them in the hall
Some years ago I knew a lad
Who greeted me with accents glad
But now he's past his thirty-five
Though thankful to be well and alive
He's neither heart nor time to sing
The music of the former sings
But let him chanticleer his own
And singing ne'er will be alone
But sister spirit come relate
What you begun at Murdo's gate
That by cockcrow I know it all
Tomorrow night I join the ball.

# *from* First Minstrel

'Mong Sydney scenes my tale begins
Sydney child of the glacier
Nursed by the ocean.
    Here thought moves in labor;
And science, in action,
Yet Sydney is free
The pride of the sisters,
Sweet Morien and all
And fair Haligonia
Destains not to call
That timepiece of the heavens' breast
Is fobbed beyond the fading west
The crow and jackdaw seek the nest
That cozy nest in lofty spruce
The nimble swallows too retire
To dream of claypit and of mire
To dream of housewall growing higher;
    And cheerful cruise
The dog is panting by the barn
And barks at what he fancies harm
Or deft connives to slumber warm
    Behind the stove

By false announcements of the night
Calls the porter to admit
At least, one thru the door....

## *from* **First Poet**

But Beauty likes to linger in the past
And also in distant birds of passage
And sometimes graces new acquaintances
Then dissolves
But now and then we find it
Where expected as in the face
And form of Molly.
Who shall presume to portray
The healthy face?
The rainbow's self
Alone can illustrate the
Variegated congress of Nature's touches
That adorn the form
And face of lovely Molly
As o'er the piano's snow-white keys
Her whiter hands doth glide.

Her fingers like the Aurora
Playing in a ruby sky.
The western winds caress her
The eastern gales subside
When intoxicated with her breath.

'Tis now I wax so jolly.
O happy hours come often,
Come back, come soon again.
Come to me now in fancy
Realities come, entrance me
Yes, come yourself my dear.

When Upper Margaree is sighted,
Again our doubts are righted,
For in with us they wheel.
The noble John MacFarlane
Of giant mind and arm
The fertile Angus Gillis
And Rory MacDonnell,
And Roderick MacLellan
With many more as willing.

They gaily walk along.
If some were still unlettered,
They knew the trend of farms,
And could respect their betters,
And well abstain from harm
And all were strong and healthy,
While some were somewhat wealthy;

Nor was there one
Who meant not soon
To stand by William Young,
And lovely girls
In pink ado
With costumes swell
Enrich the view.
But one was fairer far,
So Donald thought,
And he sang:—

Green grow the rashes, O,
Green grow the rashes, O,
The sweetest hours that e'er I spend
  Are spent among the lasses, O.

My father leads around our home
He sows, he reaps and thrashes, O,
But lesser sways my life so gay
  My living care, the lasses, O.

I'm dutiful to pa and ma
My daily toil, it passes, O,
Its studies hard would miss reward
  Were I denied the lasses, O.

My winsome Ellen beats them all
I know not what outclasses, O,
It may be beauty, health or mind
  At least, I love the lasses, O.

Her dress so plain, well, not that way
The make my skill surpasses, O,
Translucent of her charms' array,
O gee, I love the lasses, O.

Her voice would metaphor excel,
Her face is ruby flashes, O,
Let others praise the belles of old,
  Give me my age's lasses, O.

81

A Smile for those I never saw.
But Ellen, why, she mashes, O,
The same to me are war and peace
    If I may see the lasses, O.

Her hair, a coronet of down,
Brushed high around the dashes, O,
And what she says, is just her way,
    My daisy 'mong the lasses, O.

And when he sang his lyric thru,
I pondered on the ways of man.
We hardly judge 'twixt right and wrong,
We often end where we began.
The mutual love of either sex
Is seldom reckoned ere they come
It comes in power virtue decked
And threatens oft the wisest plans
The world is often unprepared
To meet this passion's quick demands.
The soldier sees no battle gained
Tho trophies hang at either hand
If she who met him (who knows where!)
Enlist him not in her command.

# *from* A Lovelorn Youth's Address to the Moon

Thou knowest that material progress
Rights and all, depend on
Study, labor, and agitation
If not entirely, to a great extent.
A century back
The parents were the lover's cross
Today 'tis others who butt in.
The lover's creed, his age, his means
His very looks are all in comment.
Look down pale moon
O say that she'll be true
Yes, she will
And when the trouble's over
So happy we will be
We'll dwell alone together
And then we shall be free

We'll talk and laugh together
We'll do it o'er again
For you were always new to me
Like sunshine after rain.

# *from* **A Lady**

The moon displays so bonny
The glades rejoice serene
The aspen, fir and holly
Adorn the restful scene.
The birds have ceased the lay
That eased my cares by day
But now my thoughts are Johnny
    He comes each night to me.

The sailor loves the compass
That guides his bark along
The soldier loves the rifle
That aids both truth and song.
But not a love have I
If Johnny's self be nigh
My true, my faithful Johnny
    He comes each night to me.

Ye seargeants, why delay him?
A pass, O why deny?
He'll reach you by reveille
Or by his side I die.
O morn delay thy speed
Art thou and wars agreed
To wile away my Johnny
    He comes each night to me.

The past is getting dreamy,
The future, I can't see;
'Tis me that's all, believe me,
But still I'll wait a wee.
The breezes rise and fall,
Their echoes warble all
With boding thoughts of Johnny
    He comes each night to me.

Here comes my lovely Johnny
And says 'twill soon be done

And peace is brought by triumphs
Our General great has won.
He vanquished all our foes
And now my joy o'erflows
Each day and hour with Johnny
      He comes each night to me.

# Bonny Birdie

To the tune of *Dainty Davie*

Meet me 'tween the byways twa
Bonny Birdie, charming Birdie
I'll be there whate'er befall
      My own, my dear, my Birdie.

A maid who dwells on yonder hill
Is certain cure for all my ills
And sure, I never loved until
      I met my charming Birdie.

She's barely yet apast her teens
If folks may judge by looks and mien
But 'mong our belles she's just a queen,
      My own dear youthful Birdie.

Her mouth is tinted red's a rose
Her face with warm affection glows—
I prize the morn that first I chose
      The road that leads to Birdie.

Her toilet's in the height of taste
Despite domestic cares and haste;
And O to span that artless waist—
      The tempting waist of Birdie.
Her voice is music to my ear,
At eventide the gloaming near,
And what care I who may appear
      So constant is my Birdie.

When I am nestled by her side,
How fond I wish she were my bride!
She's O so sweet whate'er betide—
      I'd die without my Birdie.

To me she's all the earth and more
In her I sight the future shore

Today I love as ne'er before
The Pow'rs that gave me Birdie.

**Note by James D. Gillis:**
The subject of the foregoing was Mary Jessie Ann Dunbar (better known as Birdie Dunbar). Both she and Mr. Gillis were youthful at that time. The scene is Lake Ainslie.

*In a letter to William Arthur Deacon, Gillis wrote:* In [The Great Election] there was one Lyric (Air: Green grow the Rushes O) which with "Bonnie Birdie" to the tune "Daintie Davie." I believe "Daintie or Daenty Davie" is an old tune. In the Highlands it was long known as "Sud an gaòl a bhagad òrm &c." i.e. "Such was the love thou had'st for me:—the crane for sheep—the warmth of the blankets—That was your love & it's now evaporated." But re the Lyric & B. Birdie, I judge it & them the best of my "poetries."

Before Burns' time there was a song in Broad Scotch or English beginning "Being pursued by the dragoons" &c. &c. to that tune.

# Ruth Annie

Pronounce like Rose Annie
Tune: *Annie Laurie*

'Mong Scotsville lawns so spicy
How nice to roam at ease,
And mingle with the fairest
That warble 'neath the trees;
But arbor joys are vain,
And so shall aye remain
Compared with sweet Ruth Annie,—
She's life or death to me.

Attired in Eaton's latest
She's just a sight to view;
Her sprightly step is music,
And art attained by few
Her talk is light and free,
And healthful as the breeze
That roams the broad Atlantic,—
She's life or death to me.

O famed Canadian beauties,
How oft I think upon
The fact that you're the fairest
Of beauties wooed and won.
Then O how fine to see

That all in candour free
Proclaim you best, Ruth Annie!—
You're life or death to me.

For years you've been my study,—
I labor but to earn
A moment with Ruth Annie
Among yon shaded ferns.
Then fairest maid my glee
Is perfect joy with thee,—
O there I see Ruth Annie,—
She's life or death to me.

**Note from James D. Gillis:**
The subject of the foregoing was Ruth Annie McPhail of Scotsville. She is one of an excellent family. A sister, Mary Ann, died in the United States some years ago. She too was an estimable lady.

# Miss McKay

Tune: *Sweet Marie*

I regret to see you go, Miss McKay;
Other hearts are sad I know, Miss McKay;
But we must be all resigned,
Lest our patience fall behind;
Yet, we'll miss your face so kind, Miss McKay.

Miss McKay, can't you stay, Miss McKay,
O my heart is sad today, Miss McKay;
For your voice it was so kind
That with grief I'm almost blind
To reflect I'm left behind, Miss McKay.

But our loss is Boston's gain, Miss McKay;
You will lead in beauty's train, Miss McKay;
Uncle Sam will sing your praise—
Sing your merits and your ways,
Till you find that virtue pays, Miss McKay.

Sweet the day that first we met, Miss McKay!
'Tis a day I shan't forget, Miss McKay,
At a picnic at the lake,
Where the poet's gift awakes,
There your face my heart did take, Miss McKay.

Many a happy day we've been, Miss McKay,

Side by side like King and Queen, Miss McKay,
Can I trust that future years
Other equal types of cheer
Shall present us O so near, Miss McKay.

Now farewell a long farewell, Miss McKay,
That I'm sad I need not tell, Miss McKay,
While at heart my sorrow burns
As is wont of him who mourns
May I trust that you'll return, Miss McKay.

**Note from James D. Gillis:**
The subject of the foregoing was Christy Ann MacKay, of Scotsville, later Mrs. Duncan MacMillan. She was beautiful and talented. Two brothers served in the Cuban campaign. A brother, John, was a good scholar and an excellent reader.

## *from the novel,*
# The Pie Social
## A MODERN ROMANCE

An October night, twilight rather, an intruding moonlight compromising with a busy world who would for the moment prolong the day.

O universal day, thou art the poor man's fundamental unit or measure of time—a midnight till midnight yardstick—how full of thots and meanings the word, day. Thou beginnist at midnight again at dawn for all, in youth, for some in prosperity, and as we wish, every righteous person "has his day."

Night is but a phase of day, looming since sunset. Day merges into restful twilight and twilight into night.

However on this October twilight two top-buggies were rolling wheels towards a pie social. In the fore buggy sat a lady and gentleman, in the after buggy sat two gentlemen. The former sang songs, the most impressive being "After the Ball" and "The Red River Valley."

The overflow of Red Lake, Minnesota, the North Decotan-Manitoban Red River and Plain, and the Red River and Assiniboine meeting place present fine panoramas to the view, so does another Red River in Louisiana, at least we presume so. The chances are, that like Salmon Rivers, there are a plurality of Red Rivers, but the scenes that encased our driving quartet this twilight could hardly be surpassed. Here were in abundance,

"What we can ne'er express
But cannot all conceal."

The pie social parade was in a schoolhouse within a few rods of the public highway. An angle of about thirty degrees hypotenused from the highway to the door stoop and a head tax of a quarter with a glance at Nature's photograph was all required by the genial door consul. The after care and attention by a few voluntary hostesses set all entrants at ease and the brief period of waiting passed only too soon.

By 6.30 the crowd had all arrived. At 7.00 sharp the meeting was called to general attention or parliamentary order. But there was not much to do but receive a few suggestions, discuss the same and reject or adopt,—the crowd voting en masse. Finally the auctioneer stood, and reviewed the project. In a stimulating but sensible address he depicted the handicaps of the adolescent, that is, the difficulties of the young. He explained how many young people are mendicants at our mercy exposed to criticism, wrong or correct, guilty or not guilty, but unable to resent, often poor in the midst of plenty and as history proves often head and shoulders superior to their adult tormentors, in mental capacity and public utilities.

Coming to the definite point at issue, he said, that the schoolhouse needed repairs and painting, that the teacher should be paid monthly, that stage or toy money was essential with a halfpenny and penny sample, silver shillings too, or more fresh from the United Kingdom and a (pound) bank note. Further more, picture card word matching sets, sewing punched cards, silkine, kindergarten needles, colored chalk, plasticine clay, sand, an organ or at least a gamut toy piano were desirable together with a library so chosen as to afford alternately amusement, relaxation and information. The latter, he thot, should include booklets on carpentry, tailoring, engine operation, profitable but honest labors and the systematic record of mercenary pursuits. He added that he for one was not averse to hero stories, and that he himself still read Mother Goose, but why, if we dote on chivalry and hero worship let us be the heroes of the present and begin at the schools.

He voiced an urgent appeal to the foresight and generosity of all suggesting withal application for a sub-target gun. Some cried, "Hear! Hear!" others "That's militarism!" "No!" said he, "but it's safety first and common sense and the highest genius saws by the mitre box of crisp common sense."

He raised a pie aloft, the bidding was enlivening. The gavel vamped or chorded the tuneful price nine dollars. "Well done, boys!" said the auctioneer, "I'm proud of you!" The next was a cake, the third was a box, containing not only edibles but also some fine cigars. The next was a genuine pie and so forth. It is said a loose string emits no music, but here every mental cord was soon attuned to high tension—both instinct and reason—so that all were at their best and for the good, "All's for the best."

The auction over, a sumptuous table was spread. Tea, cocoa, potatoes mashed, fat beefsteaks, pies, cakes, peaches, plums and cool raspberries regaled the merrymakers. About 10.00 the dance began. For the first two hours the Scotch Four Dance occupied the platforms. In this dance two couples promenaded in file to the first part of a strathspey, danced suitable figures or steps to the second part the men in the centre facing in opposite directions, the ladies, one facing each gentleman. After a while a two-four reel tune was played which put more vim and cheerful dexterity into the forms and movements of the graceful acrobats.

Some of these dancers knew over a hundred different steps. The dance "Jacky Tar" had 12 steps, so had "The Flowers of Edinburgh," "East Neuf of Fife," "Princess Royal" etc. In the dancing schools the first lessons impressed that one foot be always on the floor, all the time. By degrees the lesson was quickened or accelerated for each step undertaken. Many steps had names, the same as the tune, "The Duke of Gordon's Birthday" (strathspey), "Knit the Rocky" (strathspey), "Lady Jemima Johnston's" and "Lady Muir MacKenzie's Reels." So adroit were some that they were known in their sport to snuff a candle laid down in the course of a step and the light and candle survived. However it wasn't dangerous as was the Highland Scotch picnic game of walking barefooted on an elevated rope and sharp spikes stuck below. But our pie social went on with alternate sights and fours. Furthermore there were a few promenades where each boy and man was to have a partner and walk march around to violin music for 4 or 5 minutes. This relaxed the dancers and refreshed the backward or those of loftier thought.

The quartet or four, with whom the story begins, joined the dance. There were some from anear and more from afar, and many danced together that were before and during that night too, otherwise entire strangers to one another. There were no introductions, nor crying of names, but for the time being all behaved as if always acquainted and on most cordial terms.

Those who had reasons for not dancing paid no attention to the dancing platforms. They had pastimes of their own and for them as absorbing and recreative as participation in the most lively or thrilling vaudeville.

There were guessing contests, the miller's march in couples to the song:

> "Jolly is the man who lives in the mill
> The wheel goes round with a right good will,
> A hand in the hopper and another in the sack
> The right steps forward and the left steps back."

# Miss Lester

Present at the function already described was the teacher. She was of medium height and perhaps would appeal to one as less tall than the average.

Her mouth was firm. Her eyes grey blue, her plenteous hair, dark. Her cheeks and in fact her whole countenance and appearance bespoke health, knowledge, tact and ambition.

It appeared that she was a general favorite and for one cause or another was known even beyond the bounds of her own acquaintance.

At the close of the entertainment, she took the floor and gave a lucid definition of education. She recognized the value of kindergarten work, the later continuation of sane investigation in all studies, yet she maintained that whereas school days swiftly pass, it is desirable to teach and to daily teach what the average youth cannot solve owing to inexperience, poverty or seclusion from the adult world.

Both gentlemen of the after buggy with whom we began, were agreeably impressed by the teacher. Her beauty and style were not all. Her fully assimilated and developed knowledge, her ample ambition, her probable propensity to co-operate with the possible, gave her a presence that, just that, that something that people crave but cannot exactly define....

Two or three years after there was a summer picnic. The labors, sports and aspects of winter had long lost their charms and one and all hailed the Union Jack as ardently as their forebears did the Royal Flag on Braemar. — Waft in air, great Flag, let truth and honesty be thy dazzling symbol, blend modern invention and improvement to the old to enhance the present, let no foolish and weak Jewish, Latin, or Greek codes confirm us in foolish ways, lead us to surpass the highest done in any age in virtue and all its kindred labors and achievements.

J. Logan and B. Robindale, his chum, went to the picnic. The band was going merrily about 7.00 a. m. After the usual greetings, felicitations etc., the dancing platforms were cried open.

Pairs of violinists unisoned by soft caressed pianos sprang up into musical being, at some places, pairs of sturdy pipers soon arose on other pavilions, the canopy seeming a dampening reflector of floor inspiring vibrations.

Conspicuous in the dance is Farquhar MacGriffin. Entering the ring, he stands on one foot and raises the other and letting the ankle joint loose and limber he shakes his lower leg violently. Puts this foot down and repeats a similar exercise with the other. Then he invites a girl to dance with him, another couple rise opposite. The pipers play, "Athole Cummers," "Maggie Cameron," "The Hurdle Race" and Farquhar keeps time with the music, dancing most beautiful steps from the "Flowers of Edinburgh," "East Neuf of Fife," "Whistle O'er the Laveo't," and "Jack Tar" steps with the reel time. His head and shoulders erect, his hands and arms not rigid but moving naturally, his face not smiling but beaming pleasure, he was the cynosure of many eyes.

The picnic was the first ever on that spot. An eastern sun

and western moon calmly beamed for its dawn, while a western sun and eastern moon smiled on its end....

# *from Oral Tradition*

*THE FOLLOWING SHORT POEM was apparently never published. Still, all who heard it—and all who hear it— find that it remains with them, often with slight variations. The story goes that it was first recited by James D. Gillis at a dinner, a meeting of the Canadian Authors Association, honouring the birthday of Queen Victoria. Gillis was one of many dignitaries in the banquet hall, the guest of Senator Little Danny MacLennan of Inverness; and the moderator for the evening was naming the guests, one after another. He eventually pointed out James D. Gillis and was about to move on—but Gillis quickly rose to his feet, announcing, "I have composed a poem for the occasion." The room fell silent. And Gillis began: "All hail, Victoria..."*

> All Hail, Victoria
> Arrayed in her regalia
> With one foot in Canada
> And the other in Australia,
> Showering her blessings
> Upon her grateful subjects....

# Writings About

## James D. Gillis and Angus MacAskill

G ILLIS HAD A SHORT STAY at Dalhousie [University]. His study period was terminated at his own request. James D. went off to college without being too familiar with what transpired there and after a time, finding the life not to be as active as he anticipated, he changed his mind about higher education. Accordingly, one morning he went in to the president and demanded that he be given his money back. The president was quite alarmed at such a request and after the conversation had continued a little he asked James D. why he wanted to have his money back.

"Well," said James D., "all they do here is read books and I can do that at home."

—Judge Leo McIntyre

Promotional photo of Angus MacAskill and a person commonly said to be
Tom Thumb. More likely, this composite image is of Col. Nutt.

# A Sketch in Verse
## of the Feats and Exploits of Angus MacAskill, The Cape Breton Giant

Lauchlin MacNeil

Come all ye Canadians, wherever ye may be,
I pray you pay attention and listen unto me,
While I will sing the praises of a great and noble man,
Reared in fair Cape Breton, at a place by name St. Anne.

He was a true born Highlander, MacAskill was his name,
In size and strength he had no match and always put to shame
All who dared to try him, sad but wiser went away,
With reason to remember him until their dying day.

A famous fighter of renown, a monster of a man,
One day appeared, both fierce and rude, in beautiful St. Anne,
To fight and beat MacAskill brought the braggart to the town,
To deprive him of his laurels and glorious renown.

He being an upright gentleman, he stepped up to the man,
Addressing his antagonist, he shook him by the hand,
His fingers snapped, his palms were smashed, and roaring
        with the pain,
He stepped aside, his face to hide, he never smiled again.

While pulling up a heavy boat, by a crowd of stalwart lads,
MacAskill was requested to lend a helping hand;
As they were bent to test his strength, they all pulled back for fun,
But when the boat began to crack they all left on the run.

He gave a ponderous pull and lo! the boat was torn in two!
When torn apart, he took his half and left it in a pool,
He had the laugh and all the fun, to see them run away.
His deeds have weaved for him a wreath which time
        shall ne'er decay.

Our hero could lift two barrels of pork, one underneath each arm,
And carry them with apparent ease, to his store
        at his beautiful farm;
What seemed most wonderful of all was nothing more than play
To our hero, Giant MacAskill, in his young and happy days.

# THE CAPE BRETON GIANT

His horse once got disabled while plowing up a field,
The horse he soon untackled, his place straightway he filled,
And neighbours who were there declared, as he the traces catched,
The horse remaining in his trace, he fairly more than matched.

While drinking with his friends one day, while staying in New York,
He struck a puncheon just a blow, and upwards goes the cork,
He lifted up the puncheon, placed the bung-hole to his mouth,
And took his drink midst cheers of friends and
      wondering crowds about.

The greatest feat on record, performed by any man,
Was the shouldering of an anchor by our hero of St. Anne;
The anchor weighed two thousand five hundred pounds, but oh!
It was a fatal feat for him which filled his heart with woe.

It was at a pier in New York, midst the cheering of the throng,
Walking with the anchor, when he went to throw it down,
The fluke hooked in our hero's back and wrecked
      his stalwart frame;
But his name and deeds shall ever live all on the list of fame.

Our hero's height was eight feet tall, and weighing
      five hundred pounds,
Four feet between his shoulder blades, and six encircled round.
One foot ten inches was the size of boot our hero wore,
A giant indeed, such as we read in tales and ancient lore.

He had with him while travelling, a man by name Tom Thumb,
A miniature of humanity, a fellow full of fun;
At every town and city the people came in crowds
To see the giant with Tommy in his pocket lying down.

To see the giant extend his hand for Tom to dance upon,
When Tommy, always trim and gay, would dance away like fun;
Then leaping off, pretending he was spoiling for a fight,
Telling Giant MacAskill he could thrash him left and right.

While he was in London he very soon became
The object of much wonder, he won respect and fame,
Receiving marks of great respect from her Majesty the Queen,
Who gave him, made to order, two splendid golden rings.

Beside our hero's size and strength, he was a valiant man,
A credit to Cape Bretoners, who love their native land;
Noble-minded, kind and free, his deeds shall ne'er decay,
He was the noble Washington and the Wallace of his day.

# Charles Dudley Warner
# on the Giant

THERE IS ONE PLACE, however, which the traveller must not fail to visit. That is St. Ann's Bay. He will go light of baggage, for he must hire a farmer to carry him from the Bras d'Or to the branch of St. Ann's harbor, and a part of his journey will be in a rowboat. There is no ride on the continent, of the kind, so full of picturesque beauty and constant surprises as this around the indentations of St. Ann's harbor. From the high promontory where rests the fishing village of St. Ann, the traveller will cross to English Town. High bluffs, bold shores, exquisite sea-views, mountainous ranges, delicious air, the society of a member of the Dominion Parliament—these are some of the things to be enjoyed at this place. In point of grandeur and beauty it surpasses Mt. Desert, and is really the most attractive place on the whole line of the Atlantic Cable.

If the traveller has any sentiment in him he will visit here, not without emotion, the grave of the Nova Scotia Giant, who recently laid his huge frame along this, his native shore. A man of gigantic height and awful breadth of shoulders, with a hand as big as a shovel, there was nothing mean or little in his soul.

While the visitor is gazing at his vast shoes, which now can be used only as sledges, he will be told that the Giant was greatly respected by his neighbors as a man of ability and simple integrity. He was not spoiled by his metropolitan successes, bringing home from his foreign triumphs the same quiet and friendly demeanor he took away; he is almost the only example of a successful public man, who did not feel bigger than he was. He performed his duty in life without ostentation, and returned to the home he loved, unspoiled by the flattery of constant public curiosity. He knew, having tried both, how much better it is to be good than to be great. I should like to have known him. I should like to know how the world looked to him from his altitude. I should like to know how much food it took at one time to make an impression on him; I should like to know what effect an idea of ordinary size had in his capacious head. I should like to feel that thrill of physical delight he must have experienced in merely closing his hand over something. It is a pity that he could not have been educated all through, beginning at a high school, and ending in a university. There was a field for the multifarious new education! If we could have annexed him with his island, I should like to have seen him in the Senate of the United States. He would have made foreign nations respect that body, and fear his lightest remark like a declaration of war. And he would have been at home in that body of great men. Alas! he has passed away, leaving little influence except a good example of growth, and a grave which is a new promontory on that ragged coast swept by the winds of the untamed Atlantic.

I could describe the Bay of St. Ann more minutely and graphically if it were desirable to do so; but I trust that enough has been said to make the traveller wish to go there. I more unreservedly urge him to go there, because we did not go, and we should feel no responsibility for his liking or disliking. He will go upon the recommendation of two gentlemen of taste and travel whom we met at Baddeck, residents of Maine and familiar with most of the odd and striking combinations of land and water in coast scenery. When a Maine man admits that there is any place finer than Mt. Desert, it is worth making a note of.

from *Baddeck and That Sort of Thing*, 1874

The MacAskill homestead, Englishtown, St. Ann's Bay

# The Song Fishermen's Contest

*IN 1929, THE NOVA SCOTIA WRITING GROUP that called themselves The Song Fishermen sent out a call for contributions to a contest inspired by this suggestion in James D. Gillis's* The Cape Breton Giant:

*"The boat exploit would be a very choice subject for a poem. Possibly the day will arrive when one of our poets will weave a wreath of poesy about that boat, a large, lettered wreath so worded as to spell the immortal name, Angus MacAskill."*

*The submitted poems were published in the June 23, 1929, edition of* The Song Fishermen's Song Sheet, *many with comments by James D. Gillis. The winner was Cape Bretoner Stuart McCawley for his poem "You Can't Take Your Fun Off of Angus."*

THE SONG SHEET WISHES TO THANK James D. Gillis for the privilege of using the boat incident (or exploit) from *The Cape Breton Giant.* The greatness of his work will be attested by the differing points of view from which the sons and daughters of our Nova Scotian Muse have dealt with (or dwelt upon) the matter.

His comments are carefully considered and at times verge upon the essay, in discernment and critical references. His scholarship is apparent and real. We are all greatly in his debt for his kindness and trouble taken in a (for him) busy period. May we all bear in mind his advice and especially his definition of the good poet as the "entertaining steersman."

As for the contest itself, its very success has almost been its undoing. The brilliance of the contributors has been the confusion of the judges. They differed so widely in their choice, that to bring their views into any sort of agreement was conceived an utter (or stark) impossibility by those editorially involved in this hazardous (not to say foolish) undertaking.

The local grasp and tang of Stuart McCawley, the magnificent balladry of Effie Barnes, the profundity of Andrew Merkel, the superb Celticism of Michael Currie, the Miltonic vision of

Ethel Butler, the apocalyptic scope of Joe Wallace, even the destructive poison-gas of Bob Leslie,—all these witness the peculiar inspiration inherent in James Gillis' succinct description of this simple yet strong (or heroic) incident.

The prize is given to Stuart McCawley whose poem ("You Can't Take Your Fun Off of Angus") was direct, strong, idiomatic, racy, and characteristic, in the sense of being true to the character of the place, the things and the people. The single phrase "he kicked a good stance in the kelp" alone proves he is master of the technique of pulling (or pushing) a boat, besides being more than a hint at his (the poet's) prowess as a golfer.

We therefore donate to Stuart McCawley the prize and crown him with the dulse.

# You Can't Take Your Fun Off of Angus

### Stuart McCawley

Angus the Big
Was a young McAskill!
A rip-roaring, tearing rascal,
Full of the devil, full of fun,
He tipped the scale at a quarter ton;
Eight feet in his socks,
Black curly locks,
A torso of iron,
The heart of a child,
Gentle and loving,
A terror when wild.

He wasn't a giant,
He wasn't a freak,
Just a braw Scotch Laddie,
Humble and meek;
Reared in the north,
Where the winds are strong,
And nature's toughness
Makes folks shun wrong;
He loved to work,
He loved the kirk,
And for a bit of fun
He wouldn't shirk.

To this big handsome boy,
A plow was a toy,
Any stump that two oxen would back at,
He would yank out with ease,
Then fall on his knees
And thank God for his strength,
For his farm, for his trees.

He fished and he farmed,
He sang and he yarned,
He earned for his kinfolk
And loved them.
A pound of loose tea in one hand you might see,
And a brig's iron anchor he'd bend o'er his knee.

When the herring are schooling in the May-time,
Ere dawn's glow has baptized the bay,
The "Down-Northers" are hauling and loading,
Well started away for the day.
The spring tides are tearing the bottom,
And shifting the sands of the sea,
'Tis some job to run up a landing
Or beach your boat to the lee.
The McLeods from the shadow of Smokey
Thought they were first to come in,
When one of the crew saw a wonderful view
To the tune of a wonderful hymn;
Angus was hauled up on the Dingwall,
His scathans all carried ashore,
Ready for gutting and pickle,
The nets neatly hung on the shore,
Singing and chanting and stretching,
Hugging the mountains and sun,
Bubbling over with ardor,
Itching for fun.

"Whist!" said Long Rory,
The McLeod skipper's son,
"There's Big Angus,
Let us take off some fun!"
"You Alex Red Sandy,
Bide him for the hauling,
And when he gets set,
Let us all jerk away
And tumble the big one
On his back in the sea."

The wind winged their whispering to Angus,
And he smiled as he waded to help,
Upstanding and bold, to the bow he took hold,
And kicked a good stance in the kelp.
"Now shove you McLeods,
While I haul,
And we will land her over the sand,
I know you are strong,
And the push isn't long,
If everyone gives a true hand."

At the heave and the strain,
The McLeods "braced again"
(With the ebb of the tide giving help to their side)
Not a foot or an inch did they budge her,
For McAskill was having his fun,
(He enjoyed their grunting and grouching)
Then he took a fresh grip
Of the bow of that ship,
And tore her in two,
Left the stern with the crew,
And ran up the strand
With the prow in his hand.

He laughed till the sheep on the mountain answered,
And the birds in the birch joined the strain,
Even the game in the brush were joyful
Never such mirth we hear again.

## Note by James D. Gillis:

"A good stance in the kelp" is an excellent phrase, shows vision, shows clear grasp and command of the common idioms.

"Not a foot or an inch." Very deep and apt. Many would pass this unnoticed or associate it only with measure units. Foot, feet, inch and inlet are also suggested. Poetry calls for that.

The last eight lines are good, too. The emphasis of the hyperbole in the last four is worthy of Virgil, — The arrow that shot a bird thru the eye, killed a second with fright and cooked a third with the heat.

# The Fishing Boat Exploit

Andrew Merkel

A ngus, when I recall the anecdote
N arrated by James D., in truthful prose,
G one thirty years, the tale revealing those
U njesting josters, grouped around the smote,
S tark, sundered ribs of that famed fishing boat,
M y senses reel. Your lusty playmates chose
A Tarter for their sport. And you uprose,
C atapulting or semi-circling the works.
A ngus, such feats are gone, and done, methinks.
S adly the world admits a slow decay.
K eelsons are kindling-wood and kings are kinks.
I dly the weak remain to greet the day.
L ifting is left to cranes.—And no one drinks.—
L et everything, O Giant, be cast away.

**Note by James D. Gillis:**

This ode is very profound. The more I read it the more I see in it. The last six lines have wit and humor but they are clearly the work of a progressive person who performs his (or her) part, sees defects in the passing scene but abstains from propaganda.

# The Fishing Boat Exploit
## A Ghost Song of the Cape Breton Giant

Ethel H. Butler

A song! not sung at calm of twilight hour,
N or as the dawn slips o'er the quiet hills;
G iants would choose to sing, in their great pow'r,
U nheard by human ears, a song that thrills
S ouls of the Dead! 'Tis thus MACASKILL sings!...
M idnight! a storm whose billows crash in tears
A gainst the gleaming rocks! a bell buoy rings!
C ruising the waves a mighty boat appears,
A ngus, the Giant of St. Ann's, has hand
S inewy, deep-veined, upon the bending oar;
K nit are his beetling brows; no sight of land
I s sought; content to ride far from the shore,
L aughing, and thunder rolls! smiling, and lo,
L ightning reveals a chasm far below.

# THE CAPE BRETON GIANT

A chasm far below where dead men sleep;
N o fear this Giant holds of his dead peers;
G utteral his voice rolls o'er the surging deep,
U ttered in words unwashed by weakling tears...
"S ouls of the Dead! hear ye, the song I sing,
M acAskill, Giant of St. Ann's! O hear,
A nd heed.... In days gone by (loud ochees, ring!)
C rafts that were used were strong, built of the sear
A nd stalwart trunks of mighty trees, hewn, hacked.
S awn in great lengths to suit the length of limb...
K edge-anchored?" (loud the Giant's laugh!) "I packed
I dly, a boat upon my back, sang hymn,
L aus Deo, for my great strength, and strode,
L ight-laden, through the billows to the road!"

"A ne twilight eve, the boat, of extra weight
N eeding prodigious strength to beach, defied
G reat hulks of veterans! They lay in wait...
'U se your iron fist, Angus,' to me, they cried.
S miling, I gave a hand, and seized the prow.
(M en like their joke.) I hauled, and they hauled back
A gainst my strength, thinking their might, their "scow,"
C ould triumph o'er the Giant to his slack!
A ponderous pull! the boat was torn from stern
S traight to its prow! They sprawled like jelly fish,
K elp wreathing round their hollow heads! ...A turn,
I bore the boat's great half (they had their wish)
L ocked in my 'iron fist,' and flung it high,
L anding, to shiver on its keel, and die!"

A song! the morning breaks...O Youth! O Sage!
N ow bow your knee in prayer, where'er you are...
G reat Giant, did you, on your vast pilgrimage
U se as candle-flame the mightiest star
S hining within the firmament of God?
M ethinks your lofty spirit rose in flight,
A nd far above the grassy mound where trod
C omrades to bid farewell, beyond the night,
A Giant Heart to Eternal Dawn laid siege!...
S t. Ann's! O blest the bay where wild waves mourn
K eeping their solemn requiem for the liege
I mmortal soul of him, who in that bourne
L ong years ago, lived pure, and strangely strong,
L ives, for all hearts, forever in your song.

**Note by James D. Gillis:**

When I wrote *The Cape Breton Giant* I meant of course a good poem about the exploit not necessarily spelling the Giant's name. This poet literally thrice fulfilled the conditions, including a poem, second I believe to none as poetry. I would likely accord him or her first prize. There are many who could compose doggerel that would spell the name. But this is pure poetry.

This poem resembles Dr. Johnson's writings, poetry, etc. I think the writer has the vision of Milton easily. I am glad to have lived *to see* and know what I for some reason believed, that this generation could more than compete with the best of them.

Poetry calls for true wit and humor, sense (I mean a power to sense conditions or situations) and wisdom or useful information. The poet is like an entertaining steersman who pleases us and guides us through the course, his eye ever on the point.

## Laureation
# That Fishing Boat Exploit

### Katherine F. MacDonald

A ngus MacAskill, the Cape Breton giant,
N oted for prowess, had biceps so pliant—he
G rabbed up a fishing boat, tore it asunder,
U sing such force as made people wonder—how a
S on of St. Ann's with strength so prodigious

M ight bring retribution for a joke so insidious,
A nd they blamed soon found out, for with little ado—he
C aught one of the men on the toe of his shoe
A nd disdainfully tossed him a mile in the air,
S uccessfully describing a half circle there.
K nowing and dreading his temper and might—Angus
I nstantly put all the jokers to flight.
L ong may James Gillis sing of this "Lovely Giant,"
L ong may our praises ring to biceps so pliant.

**Note by James D. Gillis:**

After all I think this is the work of a lady. It may be the best poem of all. I believe like Macaulay he feigns the common monochroism in description. If that's so and if the hyperboles stress this it may be the best hit.

# Euchd a Bhat Lasgaich

## Michael D. Currie

A cuala sibse man diulnach
Air bheil cliu anns gach aite;
Bha e mor, bha e briagha,
Is bha e ciallach na nadur:
Bha iomadh fior bhuaigh air
Ann a stuamachd s an ailloachd:
Ach se spionnadh a ghairdean
A huair an cliu dha basaich.

Gur e inmadh fear laidir
'Bha St. Anns aig an am ad;
Ann a laimhseachadh bata,
Cha robh tair measg na
        bh' ann dhiu;
Ach bha Anghus MacAsgaill—
An treun gasda gun antlachd—
Ann a spionnadh san gaisge
Cho math ri seachdnar dham
        dream ud.

Than aig birlinn go cladach
O'n ghrund sgadain mar bh'aist
Dh'iarr iad cobhair Mhic Asgaill

Arson tarraing a bhata
Cuir Anghus a ghuala
Teann cruaidh ris an earr aic
Ach bha cach le cruaidh dishiell
A cumal stri ris an armun!

Nuair chunnaic a seod ud
Gur e spors bh'air an aire,
Leig e fhaicinn dhan comhlan
Gum bu ghorach am barail:
Nochd e spionnadh da riramh:
'Dh' andeoin iarann is darach
Chaidh am ba' ta na sgalban
A measg gamnihaich is talamh.

Mar bidh cridhe caomh coibhneal
Ann an com an t-sar dhiulnach,
'S gun gabhadh e ardan
Ri nabaidh le diumbadh:
Na m bualadh e lamh air,
Bhidhidh am bas air a ghiulan:
Cha dianadh lighichan sta dha:
Bhidh' e lathair na Contas!!

Translation by M. Campbell

Have you heard of the champion / Who was renowned everywhere? / He was large, he was handsome / He was wise in his nature / He had many real virtues. / He was sober and handsome. / But it was the strength of his arm / By which he will be always remembered.

There was many an able man / In St. Annes at that time / In handling a boat. / None of them was to be despised. / But Angus MacAskill / The handsome hero without a frown / In strength and in heroism / Was as good as seven of them.

There came a boat to the shore / From the fishing as was its wont / They asked MacAskill's assistance / To haul in the boat. / Angus put his shoulder / To the stern of the craft, / And the rest with strong effort / Seemed to help it ashore.

When Angus had noticed / That it was sport they had in mind / He made it known to the crowd / That their intentions were foolish. / He made manifest in earnest. / Notwithstanding iron and oak / The boat was soon in splinters / Amidst sand and clay.

If a heart full of kindness / Hadn't been in our hero's bosom / And that his temper should be roused / Against neighbor or friend / Should he strike with his hand / Death the result would be. / No doctor could help him / He would be rendering his account.

## Translation of "Euchd a Bhat Lasgaich" by James D. Gillis:

1. Have you heard of this prodigy, known far and wide? He was massive and bonny, and discreet in his doings. He was sober etc. But the strength of his arms was the clearest distinction.

2. Tho St. Ann's had many a powerful man engaged in fishing and the manning of heavy boats, A. MacAskill could pull one to seven.

3. A boat lands. Angus pulls over the beach, several others resist. "Cuir" is Imperative Mood. "Chuir" is past of "put" his shoulder.

4. The boat is torn asunder, ending their sport.

5. It is well that he was of patient temperament. Otherwise he might have slapped his tormentors and no physician would avail.

## Note by James D. Gillis:

The Poet who wrote in Gaelic had an advantage over the others. In love, war or hunting the Celtic language seems to revel. In the hands of a scholarly and skilful poet, or better a genius, each well chosen word has a wonderful punch and suggestion.

I don't know whether Lord Byron knew Gaelic but his "Waterloo" resembles true Gaelic poetry. Sir W. Scott knew Gaelic and his "Hail to the Chief" (Rodk. MacAlpine) resembles Gaelic poetry.

The gentle steady stream of W. Ross never overflowed nor tore its banks. Ross did everything right. In a controversy with a poor woman (imaginary) he left the last two stanzas to her.

If this poem was composed by a person who learned Gaelic by private study etc., it might be classed a wonder.

At any rate it is the best I've seen for some time, and slightly suggests Wm. Ross of Skye towards the end. But there's no plagiarism.

# Song of the Boat
## Molly Beresford

A cruel traitor was this Angus mor,
N ever was blacker treachery by any done;
G iant body had he, but dwarf heart it bore,
U nto all the world now be its smallness known.
S afely I sped with him over the swift wave,
M orning and evening for him braved the billowy steep,
A t dawn or at dusk to him loyal service gave,
C arrying him about his business on the deep.
A traitrous master proved this Angus mor,
(S mall and narrow was the soul of him all his days)
K now you he marred me, tossed me broken on the shore,
I can go seaward never, never more,
L eft useless, helpless, where the salt tide never strays...
L ord, do Thou judge him who...his friend...betrays!

Note: We regret this poem was received too late to be forwarded to Mr. Gillis for his comment.

**Letter from James D. Gillis**

Dear Mr. Merkel:

I have written comments as requested. Again I must show surprise for (or at) the success of our Authors. Their writings remind me of the excellent selections of the fifth, sixth, and seventh Books Nova Scotia School Series of say 1870 to 1879. They were the pick of all English.

Nova Scotia seems to be coming again to its senses. The literature, etc. and pluck etc. resembles or surpasses what I saw in my teens, about 1880 to 1885 etc. I honestly believe our time is come again. Long life to you!

# James D. Gillis:
# A Man of Parts

William Arthur Deacon

"Here thought moves in labour"

JAMES D. GILLIS IS A MAN OF LETTERS, having published books of both prose and verse, also a text book on grammar for use in the schools, and prepared a simplified map of the world. He will soon issue his first work of fiction; and the considerable number of delighted readers he has acquired almost ensures any book written by him a reasonable circulation....

Since *The Cape Breton Giant* appeared in 1898, there has been a continuous demand for his work, requiring several editions to fill; and as this is being written I learn that still another printing is in immediate prospect, for the book gains in popularity yearly. The New York Public Library is guarding one copy, and recently a friend of mine met a man on a train who had had his bound in flexible leather that he might carry it constantly as a pocket companion, from which to refresh himself in moments otherwise idle, or at times of mental depression. Mr. William T. Allen said lately in an interview that the demand for it was "perfectly surprising." An order from Detroit came in while the interview was taking place, and Mr. Allen mentioned having recently received orders from Alaska and India. The author himself mentions correspondence from Honolulu and other distant points....

Fame had been assured by his first book, *The Cape Breton Giant*. But he had not then, nor has he yet, reaped sufficient monetary return from his books to enable him to face the future carelessly. By the time his vocational training was complete he was thirty-nine years of age. Two books were out, [*The Cape Breton Giant* and *The Great Election*] and the map was done [*Cape Breton Author's Map of the World — The 4-Pole Map*]. But ten years were to elapse after the completion of the map and before he should startle the world with another book [*The Pie Social*]. With the patience of his race, he returned to his schools, and laboured for his country in the all-important post of rural school-master for five precious years. No inspiration came to him. The initial excitement over the success of his great book had worn off. It was the Black Night of the Soul. Then, perhaps it was, that the thought first came to him which was later to be enshrined in one of his own poems:

"When Victory crowns the world applauds
When failure comes there's naught but God."

It was not failure. It was only a rest period: Fate was storing up further experience to tutor his wisdom. In 1914 the Great War broke out. Gillis had enlisted in the 94th Militia Regiment in 1894, and had held a Cadet Instruction Certificate since 1909; and had taught military drill in his schools. Like a true Scot, he rushed to the colours:

"I dote on the wars as my father before me
I dream of promotions that seldom befall."

That was not in all respects a happy experiment. The author was forty-four years old; and he had always loved personal freedom too well to be able to submit to army discipline without an inner struggle. For two years he drilled; twice he was on the point of leaving with his unit, only to be disappointed on each occasion; and finally, in 1916, he returned to civilian life.

It was far from a case of all being lost save honour. During his leisure hours in camp he had completed another book—poems this time—and on his discharge rushed off to North Sydney to arrange for publication. This *opus* was *The Great Election*.... Then, too, army life does something to a man: he cannot as a rule settle back into his niche quite contentedly—sometimes, he cannot return at all. So it was with Gillis. The compulsion to change of scene was in his blood, not to be denied. Canada's great West called him; and for the following six years he dwelt on the prairies, far from the beautiful country he had made his own between Upper Margaree and MacAskill's former home at St. Ann, thirty miles east, on the Atlantic side of the Island.

For a part of that time he was a watchman at the Robert Simpson Company's store in Regina; but the greater part of it was spent in much the same sort of teaching he had done at home....

Since his return to Cape Breton in 1922, he has put in five more quiet years teaching, broken only by a term at the Summer School in 1926 for further training. During the school year 1926-27 he taught at South Highlands, Inverness County. But these years have also borne fruit, since I am privileged to announce that another book from his pen may be expected shortly. [*The Pie Social*]....

All who have read his former work will be looking forward with keenest anticipation to the publication of the new book, that sounds so promising. It is sure to be inspiring, and he always prefers an atmosphere in which, to use his own phrase, "realities are rife...."

Shy and sensitive, he has tramped alone the roads between Broad Cove on the West Coast and North Shore, a village north of St. Ann, on the East Coast of the Island; and he knows and loves every foot of that enchanting district. As he wanders about, he calls on his many friends in the farm houses and villages, who are always glad to entertain him at a meal, or put him up for the night, both because he is well liked for himself, and because his music is always welcome.

Canny in the extreme, he never takes any one into his confidence as to his intended destinations. As the old hymn runs, he "moves in a mysterious way his wonders to perform...."

This sketch is obviously—nay, glaringly—lacking in its omission of any mention of the author's emotional life—particularly in his relations with the ladies. He never married, nor has he ever explained the reason. That his abstinence from matrimony has been due to no lack of amativeness we infer from his racial inheritance and artistic temperament. One need not cite the example of Burns to realize that it is impossible for a Scottish poet to have gone through life without being in love; and his poetry confirms this hypothesis. For a peculiar thing has happened here. Whereas in his prose, which is the language of restraint, he betrays his passionate love of the scenery of his district in many lyrical passages verging on ecstasy; his poetry, which is the language of abandon, is almost devoid of any allusion to the scenic splendours with which the poet is surrounded, and their natural place in the scheme is taken by many verses to girls in general and in particular, and to the glorification of the love of man for maid....

James D. Gillis, Teacher, rates his masterpiece, *The Cape*

*Breton Giant*, none too highly. If anything, it is the prior fame of MacAskill that he exaggerates. At the time he wrote, what he says of his hero's reputation was possibly true; but it is a truism that the world has a short memory for its idols; and MacAskill's present fame he owes entirely to the literary skills of his biographer, which is yearly spreading that fame wider and ever wider. It is fortunate that the book's appearance at the end of the last century served to acquaint the rising generation, and the hordes of immigrants settling in Western Canada, with the mighty Cape Bretonian, whose immortality is now assured.

But it is not for the sake of the giant, so much as for the author's sprightly prose, that this "life" has enjoyed a vogue extending over half a century. In this, Gillis bears a striking resemblance to Walter Pater. We read them both, not so much for the information conveyed as for the marvelously fluent English, the delightful backgrounds, and stately, philosophic reflections by the way....

[Angus MacAskill's] history inspired Gillis and got him to writing. The imagination of Gillis was inflamed by the size of his subject. He experienced hero-worship at its purest and most intense. Cultivating an heroic style to harmonize with the dimensions of MacAskill, Gillis let his genius have free play with the result that he produced the most remarkable prose work ever composed on Canadian soil.

It is fortunate that the giant's life was not more eventful, and that Gillis did not have more data at his disposal; for it is the personality of the author that counts in bellelettristic writing, rather than the theme, and the less precise his information about MacAskill, the more he had to draw from himself. Just as we read *The French Revolution* for the flavour of Carlyle, regardless of how interesting his facts may be in themselves, so we read *The Cape Breton Giant* for Gillis rather than MacAskill, and are richly repaid.

A hack might have completed the biography in two printed pages, or five at most. Gillis, using every known device of padding (and some hitherto unexploited) swelled his narrative to a grand total of ninety-five pages. Scenic descriptions, moral precepts, encyclopaedic broadsides of historical and geographical facts, and shrewd observations on a hundred irrelevant matters, help out the main thread, and, what is more important, allow the author's mind and soul a fullness of self-expression that is deeply satisfying to the reader no less than to the author. So I call Gillis artist first because his masterpiece contains a higher percentage of extraneous matter than any other book, and second because of his style—now Jamesian in its prolixity, now Stevensonian in its colloquial and conversational ease and gracefulness, but always essentially, and at its noblest, pure Gillisian and inimitable....

There is only one name for the manner in which Gillis writes—that hackneyed tag, "the grand style." He acknowledges his style to be "florid"; but of course it is more than that: under stress of the author's passion it soars like an airplane, indulges in the most difficult and dangerous manoeuvres, and always returns from these flights under perfect control. The level stretches are cleverly spaced to afford the necessary relief from the dizzy heights to which he periodically climbs by labyrinthine ways of the air, known to himself alone. For at its best, Gillis's style impresses one not so much by its altitudes as by its convolutions. It is thrilling to witness him extricate himself from some of the more tortuous constructions he enters with perfect assurance.

And like those who have employed the grand style before him, the mighty masters of by-gone ages, Gillis is only able to manipulate language as he does because he maintains a perfect gravity. Never did author turn his back more resolutely upon froth, humour and idle vanities of that sort. He uses as subtitle "A Truthful Memoir"; and one feels even a trifle repelled, at times, before the severity of which his people are capable in their most earnest moments. Yet his grim determination to tell the truth, come what may, and to put all levity aside, is the source of that secret strength that sustains him in his greatest passages.

A great critic has said that absolute originality is essential to any work of art, since, without it, the composition can only be a copy or paraphrase of the real work of art. This requisite of the artist Gillis displays lavishly on every page. Given a sentence, or even a paragraph from his work, it is impossible to guess what he is going to say next. Or if the gist of any passage were given to a group composed of I do not care what famous living authors, not one of them would express the thought in phrases anything like those Gillis himself uses. His skill as a phrase-maker is proved by the way his happier expressions now pass as current coin in the speech of the Maritime Provinces.

How does he carry himself under the burden of his great powers? With humility enough to recognize his own importance, which is surely nobler than affecting ignorance of his genius.

from *The Four Jameses*, 1927

# A Little More About Gillis

### Judge Leo McIntyre

HIS *CANADIAN GRAMMAR* is one of his more serious works and in it he sets himself up as a grammarian. He takes a critical view of the language as spoken and written in those times. As he himself says in the Preface to a later work, "This Grammar threw off many useless shackles and indefinite explanations." Along with the other things he did in this work, he invented a new part of speech or perhaps it would be better to say that he resurrected an old one. He particularly found fault with the classification of certain words as "Verbs," too. For example he said that the word "Go" is called a verb. This, said James D., is absolutely false. He then proceeds to prove his statement by taking as an example the following sentence, "I will go." In this sentence said he, "What is the person doing?" and he says that the answer is that he is "Willing." The word explains what he is doing. Then he goes on to ask a further question, "How is he willing?" and he answers this by saying that he is willing to "go." Therefore, reasons James D., the word "Go" is an adverb of manner modifying "willing." In the same book he has set forth several other ideas of his own on Canadian Grammar. It is unfortunate that the book is now a collector's item and copies are very difficult to obtain....

James D. has set out his ideas on world geography in a book called simply *The Author's Four Pole Map*. In this book he takes issue with those who have established the North and South Poles in their present positions. He admits the world to be spherical in shape but said he, by what right have the North and South

Poles been placed where they are; since the earth is a sphere the axis could have been anywhere. However, he said, to lessen the confusion he would leave both poles in their present location; but he proceeded then to give the world a new axis which was to be at the equator. This, of course, meant the creation of two new poles, one of which he called the Gillis Pole and the other the Ferguson Pole, called, as he himself so aptly puts it, after a very dear friend. Then, having done all this, he proceeded to divide the world into squares, numbering each one. Now to find one's position, said he, all you need to do is locate yourself in one of these squares, consult the author's Four Pole Map, and there you are. No longer then would we have to fuss with Latitude and Longitude.

from "James D. Gillis,"
*Cape Breton Mirror*, 1952

# A Note by James D. Gillis

I DIDN'T WRITE a Geography; but I designed a World Map to eliminate the trouble due or accruing to double curvature of Longitude lines—but A. DesBrisay (Halifax, N. S.), my Blue Printer friend, is Dead, and I have no copies for sale. Jas. D. Gillis.

from an undated note to Albert MacLeod
Collection: Beaton Institute
University College of Cape Breton

# Helen Creighton Visits James D. Gillis

OUR FUNNIEST ENCOUNTER was at the top of Mount Young over-looking the lovely valley of Lake Ainslie. James D. Gillis lived there. He was author of *The Cape Breton Giant*, and now full of years. From a distance his house looked spic and span because the sides were newly painted and ladders were up for finishing the job. From a closer view we were not too sure and we had to park outside his fence because the two driveways were blocked with spruce boughs. There was no sign of life but, when I tooted my horn, he came out and seemed delighted to see us. I explained our presence and felt he didn't quite understand but was willing to do anything. He had forgotten most of his Gaelic compositions but suggested playing the fiddle. He had vaulted the fence to talk to us and now vaulted back again, and every time we suggested a change, he would vault again.

We were set up at the side of the road but the machine might have been part of the car for all the interest he showed in it. His best fiddling days were long past but he sawed away, eyes closed, and on his face was a look of sweet content. I was working from the back seat of the car and could crouch low and have my chuckle, he was so deadly serious. Isabel had more control and signaled to him when to start and watched that he didn't stroll away from the microphone. He read from *The Cape Breton Giant* in the preface of which he writes, "I have twice been to Boston. I do not say so for the sake of boast." He read also from *The Great Election* and his poem, *Miss MacKay*, accompanying it by picking on his violin strings as he recited,

> Miss MacKay, dear Miss MacKay,
> Why did you go away Miss MacKay?

James D. Gillis is part of Nova Scotia's history, and perhaps these records will have little value except in the province where he had many friends. He is written about in *The Four Jameses* by William Arthur Deacon. I once watched Halifax artist Ruth Wainwright do a pencil sketch of the back of his head, all she could see from where she was sitting. It was a noble head. Had he possessed a sense of humour, he might have been a genius.

from *A Life in Folklore,* 1975

# My Correspondence with James D. Gillis

Barbara Grantmyre

MY CORRESPONDENCE with James D. Gillis began in the summer of 1944 when I wrote to ask for his autograph.

*Dear Mr. Gillis,*

*Occupying as you do such a unique place in Canadian letters I trust you will pardon my temerity in writing to you but I have long been an admirer of your work and should like to add your autograph to my modest collection of Canadiana.*

*Although I am a housewife with a husband and four children I do a certain amount of writing. During the past three years the* Montreal Standard *has published a dozen or more of my mystery stories and has accepted another, "Poison's Indigestible," for publication shortly. But one can hardly hope that the author of so many noteworthy* belles lettres *as yourself will have cast an idle eye upon them.*

*To facilitate your reply I enclose a stamped, addressed envelope. With apologies for intruding upon your privacy, I remain*

*Your sincerely, Barbara Grantmyre.*

Within a few days I received his reply, written on a half sheet of foolscap in a bold, flourishing hand.

*Melrose Hill, Inv. Co., N.S. July 20, 1944*

*Greetings!*

*And I thank you for your compliments plus encouragement. To write (or compose) didactic mystery stories in this present age of research, analysis and dissection is no easy task, whereas the author feels duty bound to sustain curiosity and interest on the part of the Reader. That you "carry on" despite house and family suggests the memory of Napoleon I, who had the faculty of Concentration, and, as he said "could open and use one drawer and close all others" until the work was thought or done. With due respect, I subscribe my autograph.*

*Yours truly Jas. D. Gillis*

*Author of* C. B. Giant *(1898) and a few more*

117

Over the years we exchanged letters and cards. He was interested in my writing career and at odd times I sent him copies of magazines in which my stories appeared. He had been living alone at Melrose Hill but in the '50s he went to the Alderwood Rest Home at Baddeck. This letter dated March 20, 1956 came from there.

*Mrs. Grantmyre; I have read and read your Letter with admiration, interest and pleasure. I congratulate you on your success and prestige in literature. I don't write for any magazine or newspaper. I don't essay biographies etc. Occasionally I sell by mail 3 or more copies of "The Pie Social," "A Maritimes Life" and "My Palestine Pilgrimage" the only booklets (or books) from my pen whereof I hold copies. I price them 25 cents each delivered.*

*Baddeck Village (or town) is a pleasant one and the people are faultlessly pleasant etc. but I sometimes regret I left Melrose Hill (Mt. Young) and sometime I may return thereto.*

*Any time that you have leisure please write. Indeed I am glad of your success and recognition by MacLean's.*

*Yours etc., James D. Gillis*

I was delighted to learn that copies of his booklets (or books) were available and sent him a little more than the sum he asked to secure each title.

He sent this letter on May 10, 1956:—

*Alderwood Rest Home, Baddeck*

*D. Friend,*

*I thank you for the Remittance; and am mailing you copies of the mentioned books.*

*If convenient please send me a "photo" of yours. A picture would be pleasing and Mrs. Hart would be glad to see it. She is the Matron here. She is interested in your writing.*

*Yours etc., Jas. D. Gillis*

The books when they arrived were a delight. To quote the opening words of a reviewer in the *Halifax Chronicle* when *The Pie Social* was first published "James D. Gillis has done it again! I didn't think he could equal *The Cape Breton Giant* but he has."

James D. Gillis did it again in *A Maritimes Life*.

Though he didn't boast about it, most of us know that James D. had been to the United States more than once. Few know that he traveled farther afield.

In January, 1935, after paying $233.35 for a Round Trip, Third Class Ticket, Halifax to Palestine, he sailed on the *Duchess of York* for the Holy Land. He took with him a telescope, pocket compass, camera and a large diary. On his return March 30 the entries in his diary formed the basis for his booklet *My Palestine Pilgrimage*. He also added traveling hints, historical comment, comparisons of national traits, geographical data as well as three dim photos taken by his camera and a pencil drawing, artist unknown, of the "Footprint of Christ on the Rock of His Ascension from Mt. Olivet."

Our correspondence lapsed and since he was an old man I thought he was either too feeble to write, or was dead. Then someone sent me the clipping of an interview he had given a reporter from the *Cape Breton Post*. He was now at Brook Village, Inverness County. Glad to again have contact with him I sent a note and got this reply:

*Brook Village, Inverness Co., October 11, 1961*

*Dear Mrs. Grantmyre;*

*I was glad to receive your Card etc. I thank you warmly for the Gift you sent me; Your gift and good wishes clearly show that if I were in want you'd be one of the rescuers. However, I'd rather that the* Post *didn't hint that I was rather scarce in Cash. I did not complain of any poverty to them or any other person.*

*This October weather is enjoyable; no hail, no gales etc.*

*Your kind Card agreeably reminded me of happy past Days.*

*Poor Robert Burns said in praising a benefactor, Lord Glencairn; —*

> *The mother may forget her child*
> *That on her Knee an hour has been*
> *The Monarch may forget the crown*
> > *that on his head an hour has been*
> *But I'll remember thee, Glencairn,*
> > *and All that thou hast done for me.*

*Yours etc. James D. Gillis*

I fancied I detected a trace of injured pride in this letter so I wrote at once to assure him my "gift" was a mere trifle. That since I could not visit him or bring candy or books in person I had sent the small amount so someone at Brook Village could make the purchase.

I told him, too, that in my opinion the interview was entirely to his credit. And that I had not got the impression that he was in any but the most comfortable circumstances.

Perhaps he sensed more tact than truth in my letter. Perhaps he was too tired. Whatever the reason this was the end of our correspondence for he sent no reply.

from *The Atlantic Advocate*, 1971

# A Memory of
# James D. Gillis, Teacher,
## and His School, High on the Crest
## of a Hill above Lake Ainslie

Kenneth Leslie

There was a shepherd on a hill
    Eleven sheep had he.
He led them with a gentle will
    A lovely sight to see.

He watched them go the sun-long day
    To crop the grasses fair,
And though they never glanced his way
    They knew that he was there.

He played upon his strident reed
    A tune they loved to hear,
And wonder-struck forgot to feed
    And trembled, not with fear.

And now through all the city's din
    There threads a shrill sweet sound
And through the drumming noise of sin
    The shepherd's tune is wound.

# Halifax Revisited
## A Memoir of James D. Gillis
### Thomas H. Raddall

JAMES D. GILLIS, author of *The Cape Breton Giant*, *A Canadian Grammar*, *The Pie Social* and other immortal works, was born near Strathlorne, in the lovely Margaree Valley of Cape Breton, on July 11th, 1870. It was a Gaelic-speaking community and he was known in his youth as Seumas Dubh (pronounced Shamus Doo) which means Black James, from his dark eyes and hair. In English the local people referred to him usually as "Jimmie D," and under this sobriquet he was known in Inverness County for the rest of his life.

He was one of those mental cases a shade or two removed from genius and he was by no means the self-opinionated clown that a stranger might expect from reading some of his works. By nature he was a dreamer and an eccentric, a naïve and gentle soul skilled in the music of bagpipe and violin, and his mind was stored with Gaelic legends and songs and ballads. Two centuries earlier he would have been a wandering Highland bard, a welcome visitor in every bothie, and all the more respected because he seemed to be at times a little "touched."

For years he taught in a little one-room school in his native Cape Breton. Once he went to the Canadian West and taught in a small prairie school; but there the trustees objected to his original ideas and methods, there was a squabble, and he withdrew in bitterness. Once he attended Dalhousie College, but not for long. He was not qualified for matriculation, even in those easygoing days, and he found the professors too dogmatic and impatient for his taste. He withdrew in bitterness here also, and cherished a mild grudge against Dalhousie as long as he lived.

In the 1920s, when teaching standards were rising rapidly, his friends persuaded him to take a summer course at the provincial Normal College in Truro. This delighted the young teachers studying there, and there was a hilarious episode at the closing concert, when Jimmie D. took the part of the Pied Piper in a pantomimic production of *The Pied Piper of Hamelin*, with everyone in costume. Once on the stage playing his pipes Jimmie D. refused to come off, marching up and down the stage and playing every tune from "Cock o' the North" to "Miss Drummond of Perth." As a production of *The Pied Piper of Hamelin* the show was ruined, but as a production of Jimmie D. it was a howling success. Sam Campbell, who was one of the young teachers taking the course, related the whole thing to me afterwards, and I made it the basis of a favorite short story of mine, "The Pied Piper of Dipper Creek."

Eventually in the late 1920s or the very early '30s, the Department of Education retired Jimmie on a pension, and he withdrew to his small shack on Melrose Hill, Inverness County. There he lived in a state of comfortable uncleanliness and saved enough money to fulfil a lifelong dream, a trip to the Holy Land. This took place in 1936 and he described it in his booklet *My Pilgrimage to Palestine*, published by the Herald Print, North Sydney, N. S. (What he does not mention in this work is the episode at Halifax, when the port sanitary officer obliged him to take a bath before landing. This disgruntled him, and much of his dissatisfaction with the CPR, through which he had booked his whole trip, sprang from it.)

During the 1920s and early '30s a group of Nova Scotia poets used to foregather every summer and take a trip about the province, sometimes by car, sometimes by boat. It was their merry custom to hold a "poetry contest," in which each composed impromptu verses on a chosen theme, and the winner was "crowned" King (or Queen) at the end of the spree. Robert Norwood was the leading spirit of the group, and amongst others there were Stuart McCawley, Evelyn Tufts, Andrew Merkel, Robert Leslie, Kenneth Leslie, Ethel Butler, Bliss Carman and on occasion Charles G. D. Roberts. They called themselves The Song Fishermen, and Merkel used to issue mimeographed copies of the annual verses under the title *The Fishermen's Song Sheet*. It was at one of these affairs that Carman wrote his swansong, "The Sweetheart of the Sea."

The group adopted Jimmie D. as a sort of mascot. On one occasion they motored to Cape Breton and hunted him up on Melrose Hill. On another in 1930 they sent him travel money and brought him down to Halifax to join the most famous of their expeditions, a voyage from Halifax to East Dover in an old schooner (the "Drama") chartered for the occasion chiefly because Norwood loved her name. At East Dover they all marched ashore in two's, arm-in-arm, led by Gillis playing his bagpipes. They had a picnic meal in a field by the shore, held the poetry contest (the chosen theme being a sentiment from one of Jimmie D's published works) and Stuart McCawley was crowned King— the crown being a chaplet of seaweed. [See the winning poem, "You Can't Take Your Fun Off of Angus," on page 100 of this book.] Merkel had a small movie camera and got a complete record of the whole affair, which afterwards I saw several times. This was Jimmie D's last excursion until the year 1945.

In the early spring of that year with the war drawing to a close, Merkel suggested to me and to two others that we ought to get Jimmie D. down to Halifax. He said, "The old boy's getting on, he's 75 this summer, and this will probably be our last chance to see him. Besides, his books are famous now, and there are a lot of people who'd like to meet him and hear what he has to say."

When Merkel wrote me early in March 1945 that Gillis had consented to a trip to the city I made plans to be there for the great occasion. I had been studying the life and times of Joseph Howe. About the 15th of March my wife and I took a walk along the Port Mouton road and found some early mayflowers blooming on a sunny bank; and it occurred to me that my visit to the city afforded me a chance to place a few mayflowers on the grave of Howe, in tribute to the poet and the man.

And so on Saturday March 17th, 1945, I drove the hundred miles to Halifax in my old Chevrolet, with the little bunch of mayflowers, roots and all, carefully wrapped in wet cotton-wool. The Piper himself had arrived in the city the day before, with no other baggage than his precious violin and bagpipes.

Upon arrival he wore a ragged and filthy suit of hand-me-downs, a cap of the same description, a pair of badly worn shoes, an immense moth-eaten buffalo coat of a sort that I hadn't seen since my boyhood, and a pair of country-wool mittens, once white but now almost black with dirt. He had fastened the door of his abode on the top of Melrose Hill with a padlock, and for safe-keeping he wore the key dangling from one of his waistcoat buttons by a short string.

The Piper's indifference to soap and water was apparent in his person, for his face was dark with the grime of the winter's fires and his hands and nails were simply black. He must have stood six feet in his youth but now at 75 his shoulders were hunched under the weight of the years, although he walked with the long loose stride of a man of the hills and his air was eager and alert. His head was noble in spite of the grime, a large and long bald dome with a fringe of shaggy white hair at the back. The brow was full, with a pair of thick black eyebrows. His eyes were a dark and glowing brown, intelligent, kindly, the eyes of a philosopher. Beneath a keen aquiline nose was a clipped grey moustache that ran over the whole upper lip with a downward droop at the corners. His teeth had gone with the years; only one was visible, a great discolored snag in the lower right side of his mouth, and for the lack of the rest his speech was a little difficult to follow at times. His cheekbones were hairy, the chin pointed. His hands were long, with lean bony fingers. Altogether he was a striking personage.

Owing to the wartime scarcity of hotel accommodation Merkel had provided a room for the Piper in the offices of the Canadian Press on Granville Street. He had installed a cot, bedding and so on, and there was a toilet with washing facilities adjoining. Here Jimmie slept during his stay. He used the toilet but ignored the washing facilities with the scorn of a man accustomed to the rugged life of Melrose Hill.

Merkel was treasurer and indeed the leading spirit of the reception committee, which otherwise consisted of Roy Lawrence, Jim Martell and myself. The first job was to get the old man a decent suit of clothes, with shirt, collar, tie, boots and so on. It was a delicate business, for the Piper had his pride, God bless him, but we managed it. The suit we suggested was of light brown shade, the shirt and tie khaki, and we got him a large tartan scarf which he liked to wear with its ends tucked inside his jacket. For footwear after some deliberation he chose a pair of rubber sea-boots of the half-Wellington sort, and these he wore with the tops tucked up under his trouser legs. We also provided the old man with pocket money and suggested a haircut for a start. The clip, and the shaving of the neck beneath, left a conspicuous band of clean skin above the collar. If he ever washed his hands it was a momentary sluicing under a tap, for the ingrained darkness remained. When eating he would cut up his food with fork and knife, lay these now unnecessary tools aside, and pick up the food and pop it into his mouth with his fingers.

On the afternoon of his arrival (March 16th) Merkel took Gillis to the Provincial Archives and introduced him to Jim Martell, who showed him about the place. Two reporters were there from the Halifax dailies. They questioned him eagerly about his home and his visit, and wrote in their columns the next day a very fine account of "The Sage of Melrose Hill."

On the following day (Saturday March 17th) we got the Piper fitted out with new clothes, and that evening we gathered at Merkel's house, 50 South Park Street, for a musical evening. Jim and Olga Martell were there, and Roy Lawrence, Professor Wilson of Dalhousie, Pauline Barrett, Bob Chambers and wife, Laura Carten, Tully Merkel and her two daughters, a few others whose names I don't recall. We talked for a time about Cape Breton, and discussed with the Piper his various works; but chiefly the evening was given over to Jimmie D. and his music. He asked Olga to "make chords" on the piano for him, and with the aid of these he tuned his fiddle and pipes and strode up and down the long parlor for half an hour at a time, pausing only to explain the name and nature of each piece. At my request he played "The Barren Rocks of Aden," "The Hundred Pipers" and "The Road to the Isles" as part of his bagpipe program. His pipes were very old and always a little off-key, although he made valiant attempts to "get them right." Sometimes he managed very well; they were temperamental things. The bag was covered with the dark green tartan of the MacKenzies (the Gillis family are a sept of that clan) and each of the three drone-pipes bore long ribbons and bands of the same tartan. The pipes themselves were of wood and ivory, the ivory yellow with the age, and the wood was from a hard black African tree, the best for bagpipes, Jimmie said. Once started on the pipes the old man was hard to stop (as they discovered at Normal College) and we were afraid he would overtire himself. But in fact he seemed to gain strength as the evening went on. Finally, since it was St. Patrick's Day, we asked him for a tune in honor of the day, and he inflated his bagpipes and rendered an Irish jig with great spirit.

Sunday, March 18th, was a miracle of a day, sunny and warm, with a soft air that belonged to May. On the shady side of the city streets the winter's ice hung on in the gutters, black with soot, but wherever the spring sun fell the ground was bare and the frost had gone. I had mentioned to Martell and Merkel my notion of placing mayflowers on Joe Howe's grave, simply and unobtrusively, and letting my little tribute go at that. Merkel and Martell would have none of it. "You," said Martell, pointing to me, "should read aloud Howe's own ode to the mayflower, right there at his grave, before you plant the flower." "And you," said Merkel, pointing to Jimmie D., "should play a lament on the pipes at the end."

So in mid-afternoon we drove into Camp Hill cemetery in two cars, Merkel and Gillis, Martell and myself. No others were present except one or two casual strollers in the cemetery. The ceremony was simple enough. I stepped up to the Howe grave-stone, took off my hat and recited Howe's ode to his favorite flower. Then, with Jim Martell assisting, I planted the mayflowers. Then, in his ragged cap and shaggy old buffalo coat (which he had in-sisted on wearing) Jimmie D. strode up and down before the grave and obelisk playing "Neil Gow's Lament." At this point I discovered that Merkel had smuggled his movie camera upon the scene and was taking a record of the whole thing. As usual Jimmie D. was hard to stop. Before long a crowd had gathered. Where they all came from, I know not. I swore to Merkel later that some of them must have popped up out of the adjacent graves. At any rate we bundled Gillis and pipes into a car and fled. Unfortunately some enterprising soul told one of the Halifax papers and there was a paragraph the next day. I say unfortu-nately because our little tribute was private and sincere and I have always shrunk from anything that smacked of the public-ity stunt. Also Dr. D. C. Harvey, Provincial Archivist (and Jim Martell's boss) reproved Jim for being associated with anything "so undignified," his chief point being that Gillis was a lunatic and laughingstock. Harvey was a humorless man, of course.

On this (Sunday) evening we gathered at Martell's house in Oakland Road—Gillis, Jim and Olga Martell, Roy Lawrence, John Lang, Pauline Barrett, Andrew and Tully Merkel, Bill Martell and wife, and the Rev. J. W. A. Nicholson. Jimmie was delighted to find in the parson a fellow Gael from Cape Breton, and they carried on a long and animated conversation in Gaelic. But most of the time Gillis entertained us with Highland music, on the fiddle to some extent but mostly on the pipes, marching up and down the room, completely oblivious of the time, of the company, of anything but the tunes that came crowding into his head. (Merkel said that in his room in the Canadian Press offices Jimmie would be heard piping away at all sorts of odd hours of the night. Wherever he went he carried the bagpipes himself. He would let someone else carry the violin on occasion but not his precious pipes. Nor would he put them down anywhere except in some spot where they were immediately under his eye. He explained gently that it was not that he distrusted people but just that he could not rest comfortably when they were out of his sight.)

During the past week or two Martell had approached the various Halifax broadcasting stations with a view to putting the Piper on the air. None were interested, but Dorothea Cox of the CBC agreed to write her head office about it. Head office replied that they would be interested only if Raddall interviewed Gillis. I said that was alright with me provided that Jimmie got the whole honorarium. (It was $20 for a 15-minute interview.) This was soon agreed, and we made an appointment to record the interview at the CBC studios on Sackville Street.

On Monday March 19th at 11 in the morning I went with Merkel and Lawrence and Gillis to the Legislature, where our guest was much impressed with the Red Room. Then Harold Connolly brought Premier A. S. MacMillan along and they had a long chat with Gillis about affairs in general and Cape Breton in particular. Here, as everywhere, the Piper conducted himself with a simple dignity that made you love him. There was nothing of the blatant egotist that many readers of his works expect to see in the author of *The Cape Breton Giant*. His egotism was that of a child, a naïve and gentle but firm belief in himself and his notion of men and things.

In the evening Gillis was guest of honor at a meeting of the Poetry Society in the library of Queen Elizabeth school. Several members of the Canadian Authors Association were present also, and others of the general public. Old Sir Joseph Chisholm, the

Chief Justice, who had long been a patron of the Poetry Society, drew me aside and asked me a little querulously if the whole thing was a joke. If so, he suggested, it was in bad taste. I told him that the poets had invited Gillis, through Merkel, because many of them had never seen or heard the author of *The Cape Breton Giant*, and this was their chance. I assured him too that our primary idea had been to give the old man a holiday in the city, and that we had found him just as eager to meet the public as the public were to meet him.

Merkel made a very good introductory address, kindly and judicious and full of truth. A Mrs. McPhail sang for us (she had a lovely voice) and a Mrs. Webber played one or two piano solos. The Piper then arose on the dais and addressed the gathering in his simple fashion, speaking of poetry in general and his own favorite poets in particular. When he discovered Poe's "The Raven," he said, he was filled with wonder and delight—"It was like finding an oil well close beside the house." He spoke easily and at length, his large brown eyes aglow, and making eloquent gestures of his lean hands. When he closed there was great applause, and Sir Joseph arose and expressed the thanks of all present. I think Sir Joe was still a little suspicious of Merkel's motive in exhibiting his "freak"; but I thing that he was agreeably surprised to find Gillis a creature capable of intelligent thought and speech, and a very well-read one, too.

After the meeting closed, Gillis, the Martells, the Merkels, my sister Hilda and I went on to the home of Mrs. Dauphinee, a member of the Poetry Society. There we found Bob Chambers, cartoonist of the *Halifax Herald*, book illustrator and artist; and later on Chambers presented Gillis with a fine pencil drawing of himself playing his beloved bagpipes. Here again the Piper rose to the occasion, entertaining the company with violin and pipes, deaf to all suggestions that he might need a rest. Until a late hour the welkin rang with his tunes.

On Tuesday afternoon I went with Gillis to the CBC studio on Sackville Street to record our interview. While we were waiting for the studio staff to get things organized we chatted with Dorothea Cox; and for her benefit, and in reply to one of her questions, Gillis got up and demonstrated with surprising agility the steps of the Highland Fling, the Strathspey and one or two others. Then we went into a small recording studio and went to work. The CBC people like to have a prepared script but in this case they had to forget all about such a thing. Gillis would have ignored the script in any case. So the whole interview was extempore. In reply to my questions Jimmie talked of his home at Melrose Hill—"close to the international boundary between Inverness and Victoria counties"—and of the beauties of Lake Ainslie, how he came to write *The Cape Breton Giant*, how to prepare the bagpipes for playing ("You soak the reeds in good rum or whiskey" etc.). And he sang a verse or two of his own "Farewell to Miss Mackay," and a verse of a Gaelic song, "Braighe Margaree," in praise of his native valley. We made two fifteen-minute records, and a further nine-minute record for use by John Fisher in his "John Fisher Reports" program.

I had managed to get some beer—a scarce commodity in Halifax in March '45—and we all adjourned or gathered in Pauline Barrett's room at the Lord Nelson hotel—Gillis, Merkel, Professor Mowat of Dalhousie, a Wren lieutenant named Gladys Finch (known to us as "Finchie"). We sat about the floor and on the bed, Pauline provided some delicious rye-and-meat sand-wiches, and we drank the beer and some whiskey that Finchie had obtained from the Dockyard officers' mess. Pauline had her radio turned on, and at 7:15 we heard the CBC broadcast of our interview.

We remained in the hotel room until midnight, smoking and chatting over the glasses. Whenever we drank, Jimmie D. gave his favorite toast, lifting his glass and saying frequently, "That we be no worse!" And he sang for us a number of Gaelic songs, explaining what they meant. There was one deliciously funny ballad about a man who drove his cart to the grist mill for a bag or two of flour, and in turning to come away backed his cart into the mill pond. And there was one with a partly English refrain that we all sang together:

> "My heart is low, pity me,
> Lonesome for my darling.
> But since she has come back to me,
> I'll sing the rest in Gaelic."

Towards midnight Merkel, Martell, Gillis, Pauline, Mowat, Finchie and I got into Merkel's car (Pauline on my lap) and drove down to the harbour by the Yacht Club. Merkel had some fine verses lately sent him by Charles Bruce from the western front, and Pauline read them aloud by the light of Merkel's electric torch. In view of the harbor water it was the proper setting for Bruce's lines, which always have the good salt taste of his Guysborough shore.

On Wednesday, March 21st, the *Halifax Chronicle's* radio station CJCH suddenly was very keen to have a broadcast of Gillis and myself, so we went to their studio on the top floor of the Lord Nelson this afternoon and did a twelve-minute recording in which Jimmie described an old fashioned Cape Breton cloth-fulling bee and sang a verse or two of the Highland boatsong "Fhear a Bhata" (O my boatman), which was much used at fulling frolics because the oar-rhythm was exactly right for the labor of lifting and thumping the raw homespun on the boards of the fulling-table. I was anxious to get this recorded because it has to do with a custom now dying or dead in Cape Breton; and for the same reason I got Jimmie to sing another fine old fulling-song, "Morag of the Flowing Hair." Morag was the old secret name, in Gaelic, for Bonnie Prince Charlie; and the song is an allegory in which Morag and her "maidens" are urged to return and beat the red cloth, i.e. the British soldiers. Jimmie sang it in Gaelic, of course. It is a rare sample of the Jacobite songs carried to Nova Scotia by veterans of Prince Charlie's army who fled from the Hebrides after the '45—almost exactly two centuries ago.

This evening F. B. McCurdy, the Halifax financier, a native of Cape Breton himself, invited Gillis to dinner. Jimmie told us about it afterwards with gusto. The dinner was one of several courses and Jimmie ate so heartily of the first two that "I was full, you understand, before it was half over." After dinner, to bring luck to the house in the old Highland fashion, Jimmie played his pipes through the house from cellar to garret, being careful not to miss a single room—F. B. leading the way, then Jimmie, then the family and the servants. Jimmie said feelingly, "My, that is a very big house. It has more rooms than a university. I did not know he was such a rich man." He and the McCurdys were having such a good time at Emscote that Jimmie forgot a promise to meet the students at Pine Hill, the theological college of United Church, not far away. However the students, not to be defrauded, sent a delegation to Emscote to claim their man, and forth he went with them. At Pine Hill he answered their questions about his written works and played his bagpipes and had a fine time of it. At the end they presented him with a purse of money and a neatly worded Gaelic inscription expressing their thanks for his courtesy in coming to them.

Early the next morning (Thursday, March 22nd) Gillis returned to his native hills via the early morning train. Tully Merkel had put up a box lunch for him and he was happy. He repeated what he had told us several times during his visit, "This is the best time I ever had in my life." Later on we collected the broadcasting fees, added some money of our own and Merkel sent it on to him. In acknowledging this Jimmie sent his own account of the visit, of which Merkel kept the original. I made a copy for myself. I only wish that we could have persuaded someone with the proper equipment to take three or four days and carefully record Jimmie's store of Gaelic songs and legends, which were so valuable and which were lost forever when he died. In the long run that would have been his best monument.

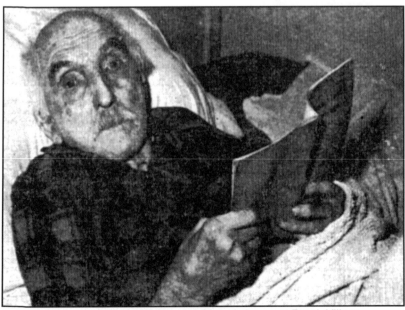

James D. Gillis at 93, in a neighbour's home at Brook Village.
From a newspaper clipping; photo by Abbass.

# EDITOR'S NOTE

JAMES D. GILLIS WROTE, "Cape Bretonians, one and all, remember that Angus MacAskill was our countryman. Remember that we have reason to be proud of him. Remember that he was one of the greatest giants the world has ever seen. Yes, one of the giants of the world was a native of Cape Breton."

And we add: Cape Bretoners, remember that James D. Gillis was also one of your own. We shall never see his like again. He preserved our Giant and he, James D., likewise belongs to the world. He was so far ahead of his time. A proud Canadian, an ardent feminist, a fighter for fairness and freedom. Let this dove of anthology fly long and high, and grant you peace.